FOUNDING MOTHERS

Profiles of Ten Wives of America's Founding Fathers

by
P.M. Zall

Washington DC
National Center for Study of the Founders

1991

First Edition
Published 1991 By

HERITAGE BOOKS, INC.
1540-E Pointer Ridge Place
Bowie, MD 20716
(301) 390-7709

ISBN 1-55613-426-6

A Complete Catalog Listing Hundreds of Titles on
History, Genealogy & Americana
Free on Request

For my sisters: Betty, Eleanor, Celia, and Ida.

CONTENTS

All portraits in this book are reproduced by permission of
The Huntington Library, San Marino, California

INTRODUCTION
FOUNDING MOTHERS

Wives of Founding Fathers

Sometimes we need reminding about such obvious facts of life as that we could not have had Founding Fathers without Founding Mothers. Biological necessity aside, somebody had to be minding the store while the heroes sallied forth forging the consciousness of a new nation. Yet whoever nowadays hears of Debby Franklin, Molly Morris, or Sally Jay? Since their spouses never served as Presidents, their gilt from associating with notable men is less burnished than that of Patsy Washington, Abigail Adams, Martha Jefferson, or Dolley Madison. Yet even our First Ladies seem celebrated as persons worthy of their own note. The present profiles or silhouettes (rather than full portraits) must serve as mere reminders that behind every great man was a woman to whom attention must be paid.

Each of the ten women profiled here took an active part in the Revolution, not as a combatant, certainly; but as a survivor of displacement, disaster, sometimes despair. To emphasize this side of the struggle, I have included a profile of a leading Loyalist wife, Grace Galloway, whose aristocratic bearing as well as the fact of her husband's villainy made her the target of revolutionary officialdom. Grace Galloway endured insult and terrorist attack alone rather than seek safety in exile and thereby lose property which properly belonged to her child. Like the other women, she selflessly sacrificed even security for the sake of family.

In an earlier age this kind of self-sacrifice could have been explained as traditional self-denial in hopes of eternal salvation. By the latter part of the Eighteenth Century, however, the old-time religion had given way to a rational religion that stressed individual reason and conscience as guides to good conduct. Reason became the arbiter in conflicts as between the natural instinct of maternal love and the acquired sense of patriotism to the new nation. These women, born subjects of George the Third, willingly risked survival in an unprecedented form of government, like a new family without a father but with elder brothers taking turns playing leader. With the exception of Grace Galloway, these women chose to follow. They did have the choice.

In the absence of menfolk in peace or war, they willingly assumed roles of husband and father surrogates. Without legal sanction they became managers. With spouse Benjamin Franklin away from home half the 44 years of their marriage, Debby Franklin had to take over his role as printer, postmaster, and *pater familias*. Women of succeeding generations with more education and culture adapted less easily to such roles. John Adams warned his daughter against showing off her learning. Thomas Jefferson ensured that his daughters would have the best education the Western World offered. His daughter Martha lived to regret that she was thus ill-equipped for life in America. In the absence of her husband, she felt helpless, a truly unAmerican way of wife.

Birthing, too, had its risks. On the eve of the Revolution a woman could expect a dozen babies by age 36; only half would reach age five. Yet half the population was estimated to be under 16. A German traveler reported that the women he met here were either pregnant or carried a child in their arms while leading one by the hand.

Ben Franklin gave this as an explanation for America's beating the British — we outnumbered them.

Nevertheless, there was loneliness. Sally Jay took her children wherever her diplomat husband, John Jay, led them, only to find that his duty at court or chancery kept him from their side, leaving them isolated, friendless on foreign soil. And even back home, his duties as Chief Justice of the United States Supreme Court meant they saw just as little of him.

Some compensation came from extended families. In Sally Jay's case, as an heiress of the Livingston clan she could always count on connections across the land. When her mother was a girl, the colonies consisted of some 350 thousand persons tied only by regional economic interests — fishing, farming, or furs. By the 1770s the nation approximated some 2.5 millions. Such extended families must have contributed to the cementing of the union.

Without pressing the point, consider how the marriage of Nancy Randolph from Virginia to Gouverneur Morris of New York made that grand old Federalist Morris a brother-in-law to Thomas Jefferson's daughter; or how the marriage of Jefferson's granddaughter into the noble Coolidge family of Boston united North and South.

Such families extended the network to embrace friendships, too. The Robert Morrises were great friends of the George Washingtons of Virginia, the John Jays of New York, and the John Hancocks of Massachusetts. This is not to suggest some sinister underground network. Comparable networks tied merchants, land speculators, or soldiers. But wives gave a sense of being united as a nation, one people with shared culture.

Elizabeth Hamilton, Dolley Madison and Martha Jefferson Randolph lived long enough to become national shrines. Foreign visitors requested to see them, Presidents came calling on New Years Day. These Founding Mothers were venerated as relics of the Founding Fathers. Surely two hundred years later they deserve honor on their own.

Sketches of a few Founding Mothers appear in standard reference works like *Notable American Women*, published by Harvard. Biographies of such superstars as Abigail Adams may be found in any public library and on some drugstore racks. But who speaks for the more obscure figures like Elizabeth Hamilton or Sally Jay? In this great age of multi-volume editions, the papers of their husbands are accessible and they include words from the wives. They can speak for themselves.

The profiles below are intended to let them tell their own stories so far as feasible in their own words. My narrative is meant chiefly to link quotations or paraphrases of their letters or reports from contemporary correspondence, with no psychoanalyzing. I have exploited the enormous holdings of books and manuscripts at the Huntington Library, my sole resource. The writers' words are their own, but I have modernized spelling and punctuation wherever needed to make them accessible for today's readers in the USA. This is true even of the extracts from their letters or other documents that follow each profile. The intent of these extracts is to add a personal dimension attainable only through sampling each woman's voice with minimum narrative interference.

These accessible books have been very useful:

For Deborah Franklin, Martha Washington, Abigail Adams, Martha Jefferson Randolph, and Dolley Madison, *Notable American Women* (Harvard University Press, 1971).

For Grace Galloway, *Diary of Grace Growdon Galloway* (Arno Press, 1971) and Mary Beth Norton, *Liberty's Daughters* (Little, Brown, 1980).

For Mary White Morris, the article by Charles Henry Hart in the *Pennsylvania Magazine of History and Biography* 2(1878)157-84.

For Sally Jay, *Unpublished Papers of John Jay*, ed. R.B. Morris (Harper and Row, 1975, 1980).

For Nancy Morris, William Cabell Bruce, *John Randolph of Roanoke* (Putnam, 1922).

Additionally for Martha Jefferson Randolph, Sarah N. Randolph, *Domestic Life of Thomas Jefferson* (Harvard University Press, 1939) and *Family Letters of Thomas Jefferson* (University of Missouri Press, 1966).

Additionally for Dolley Madison, Conover Hunt-Jones, *Dolley and the "Great Little Madison"* (American Institute of Architects, 1977).

For Elizabeth Hamilton, Allan M. Hamilton, *Intimate Life of Alexander Hamilton* (Scribners, 1910) and *Papers of Alexander Hamilton (Columbia University Press, 1961-87).*

I am grateful to the Huntington Library for permission to quote excerpts from manuscript letters or journals by and about each of the women profiled in this book.

P.M. Zall
San Marino, California
February, 1991

Deborah Franklin, from an engraving of a painting

DEBORAH READ FRANKLIN

Birthdate and place unknown. Probably Birmingham, England or Philadelphia in 1707.

Died of stroke, Philadelphia, 19 December 1774.

Second of seven children born to carpenter John Read, London, and Sarah White Read, Birmingham, immigrants to Philadelphia before 1711.

Wed potter John Rogers, 5 August 1725; abandoned December 1727. Common law union with Benjamin Franklin, September 1730.

Two children — Francis Folger (1732-36) who died of smallpox and Sarah (1743-1808) who wed Richard Bache.

DEBORAH READ FRANKLIN

All we know about Deborah Read Franklin is what her husband said, except for a handful of letters she left behind. We know she came over from Birmingham, England but not when she was born.[1] According to Franklin, they were teenaged lovers. It was not love at first sight, for she first saw him as he slouched into Philadelphia munching on one roll with two others under his arms. She thought he looked ridiculous.

He came to room at her recently widowed mother's home. Her father had been a house-builder but did not leave them much of a fortune, having been bilked out of his own

1

by a confidence man. So when teenager Franklin and young Debby asked Mrs. Read's permission to marry, she said no — not until he had more promising prospects of making a living.

It was to improve those prospects that the apprentice printer went overseas to develop his own trade in London. But dipping into those fleshpots, he sent Debby a "dear Joan" letter telling her not to wait as he did not expect to return. Her relatives thereupon fixed a marriage with a no-good potter, John Rogers. Rogers spent all her dowry then ran away with his pottery apprentice rather than face debtors prison.

Ben Franklin returned from London, set up a printing business, and looked around for a wife to share his life and work. For old times' sake, he visited his former landlady and saw poor Debby wasting away in the flower of youth. Out of pity and guilt he "took her to wife," the first of September 1730.

"Took her to wife" meant they did not have an official marriage. They were in a double bind. If they wed legally and that no-good potter John Rogers still lived, they would be guilty of bigamy, imprisoned for life after suffering 39 lashes naked in the marketplace. If Rogers had died, they would have been legally responsible for his debts. So theirs was a common-law marriage — of highest respectability since Mrs. Read, Debby's mother, came to live with them, setting up a little general store in the front of the house.

Franklin's printing shop was in the back of the house. Debby helped out in the store and in the shop, "folding and stitching pamphlets, tending shop, purchasing old linen rags" for making paper, and of course making clothes for herself and the family.[2] Besides Mrs. Read and Franklin, she also had to look after his illegitimate son, William (whose unwed, unnamed mother continued to be supported by father and son the rest of her life).

In 1755, when William was about 25 and Sarah 12, a boarder testified that Mrs. Franklin felt that her husband neglected her and Sally in favor of William, whom she therefore called "the greatest villain upon earth!" in "foulest terms" the boarder had ever heard from a gentlewoman.[2] But this was given as an instance of her "turbulent temper" rather than a manifestation of deep-seated dislike. She raised little Sally to depend upon him as a big brother and she herself, in Franklin's absence, relied on him as an only son.

Franklin remembered the early days: "We kept no idle servants, our table was plain and simple, our furniture of the cheapest. . . . My breakfast was a long time bread and milk (no tea), and I ate it out of a twopenny earthen porringer with a pewter spoon.

"But mark how luxury will enter families and make a progress in spite of principle. Being called one morning to breakfast, I found it in a china bowl with a spoon of silver. . . bought for me without my knowledge by my wife. It had cost her the enormous sum of three and twenty shillings, for which she had no other excuse or apology to make but that she thought *her* husband deserved a silver spoon and china bowl as well as any of her neighbours."[3]

What was Debby Read Franklin really like? Her husband, reporting on a trip to her native Birmingham, told her he had come across a relative who reminded him of her, like one of those old-fashioned mugs, "a jolly lively dame" with the same little blue eyes, clean and tidy, good natured and lovely.[4]

But he knew she was tough-minded and resourceful, too, for whenever he was away from home — and that totaled 25 out of 44 years of marriage — it was she who minded the store and the printing shop and the post office for all of British North America! In one of her few surviving official letters, she warned the commander-in-chief of the armed forces on this continent that he had better command his troops to stop delaying her postmen if he expected to receive any more mail from Philadelphia.[5]

Thanks to her help her husband was able to take early retirement at age 42 so he could spend another 42 years of his life doing what he liked best to do in the legislatures, courts, boudoirs and salons of the western world. By the time he went off to England as a diplomat, together they had built up a conglomerate of printing shops up and down the Atlantic coast and into the frontier, along with a wholesale paper business and one in ink, too.

Whenever an apprentice finished training they would set him up with a press, types, paper and ink as a full partner in a franchise operation like modern fast-food or instant printing businesses. This gave them the added benefit of a chain of outlets for the Poor Richard almanacs, the newspapers, and the books they turned out in Philadelphia. Serving as postmaster for the continent helped insure wide distribution.

The income along with profits from real estate ventures enabled Franklin to sell the Philadelphia printing shop to David Hall under an arrangement by which he would serve as a silent partner, sharing the profits for a number of years. Under those circumstances, Debby could be assured of an income even when he was overseas. He begged her to sail with him, but she feared the ocean more than loneliness.

They kept in long-distance touch by mail when, even for the postmaster-general of all North America, a letter took three months to get to London and another three months to be answered. "How pleased I am to read [your letter] over and over again — I call it a husband's love letter. I have wrote several letters to you, one almost every day but then I could not forbear saying something to you about [politics]. Then I would destroy it and begin again and burn it again . . . ."[6]

Her cure for loneliness was busyness. Besides taking care of business, she was trying to raise their daughter (a little boy, Francis, had died of smallpox) and look after an extended family of relatives on both sides the family. In tough times like the Stamp Act crisis, when the public thought Franklin had sold out to the British government, she had to bear arms to defend hearth and home.

"On Monday [night] last we had very great [rioting]," she reported.[7] "Several houses were threatened to be pulled down. Cousin Davenport came . . . stayed with me some time. Towards night I said he should fetch a gun or two as we had none.

"I sent to ask my brother to come and bring his gun also, so we made one room into a [fortress]. I ordered some sort of defense upstairs such as I could manage myself. I said, when I was advised to remove, that I was very sure you had done nothing to hurt anybody [and] I had not given offense to any person at all, nor would I be made uneasy by anybody, nor would I stir or show the least uneasiness — but if anyone came to disturb me, I would show a proper resentment."

As time went on she grew bolder in business. The neighborhood knew her as a tough bargainer; one neighbor called her a porcupine. She tried expanding their real estate holdings abroad: "I have [bought] the land — I believe it is in Nova Scotia or some such place." She was dealing with Mad Anthony Wayne.[8] She paid Mr. Wayne 53 pounds for the deed — "so you see I am a real land speculator. I tell Sally this is for grandchildren. She seemed very well pleased at it, and thinks we shall have some in good time."

And in due time Sally became a woman: "Sally wishes to marry Mr. Bache," a poor man with no prospects.[9] Doubtlessly remembering her own mother's reaction many years earlier, Debby did not reject him out of hand. "I treat him as a friend and shall while I am alone, for I think he deserves it. And was I to do otherwise, I think it would only drive her to see him somewhere else."

Sally did marry her young man, Richard Bache, and did bring the Franklins a grandson, Ben. She called him her "Kingbird." She confessed conversing with him at two months.[10] "My dear [Kingbird] has been atalking about you and is grown finely within these two weeks and is one of the best tempered children I ever saw and everybody says he is much like you."

Nowadays all babies look like Ben Franklin, but Debby said that when she took the baby out for an airing all the neighbors wanted to see him. "Many says he is like you and some his father." More, he shared his grandpa's love of music: When his dad sang, the baby was ecstatic. For sad songs, tears flowed down his cheeks. For happy songs, he joined in and sang along.

Grandma duly reported every tooth cut and how Sally laid the baby over her knee and gave him his first spanking as Debby looked on and said not one word. Franklin's reply praised her restraint, telling her about the two boys he'd overheard.[11] One asked why the other is crying. He had broken a bottle of vinegar "and my mother will whip me." "No she won't whip you." "Indeed she will." "What! don't you have a grandmother?" Besides almost daily reports about Kingbird and the birth of his sibling William, Debby told Franklin about local gossip, even when she's the target. "I have to tell you something you would not believe of me only I tell you myself. I have been to a play! ... I expected somebody to speak to me [about it], but I have been twice to the Presbyterian [church] — which will be worse to some folks."[12] The Franklins' church was Episcopalian.

Her last letter was still full of little Kingbird, now 4. His uncle had given him a dollar to go to the play. "His mama asked him whether he would give it for a ticket or buy his [5-months old brother William] a necklace. He said his brother a necklace. He is as charming a child as ever was born. My grandchildren are the best in the world."[13]

In this last letter could be seen the strain of the stroke she had suffered four years earlier complicated by the need to take care of business, miscellaneous cousins, nieces, and Sally's expanding family. Finally, after 16 years of committed correspondence, she concluded simply, "Sally will write. I can't write any more. I am your afeckshonewife D Franklin."

Digging the guilt more deeply, he had just written a complaining letter to her.[14] "It is now nine long months since I received a letter from my dear Debby. I have supposed it owing to your continual expectation of my return. I have feared that some indisposition has rendered you unable to write. I have imagined anything rather than admit a supposition that your kind attention towards me was abated. And yet when so many other old friends have dropt a line to me now and then . . . why might I not have expected the same comfort from you who used to be so diligent and faithful a correspondent?" She did not live to read those lines.

Two months after receiving the sad word of her death (mid- December 1774), he sailed for home. The depth of loss was unfathomable. "I have lately lost my old and faithful companion, and I every day become more sensible of the greatness of that loss that cannot now be repaired."[15]

He had sixteen more years of greatness to get through. While negotiating the treaty with France that would bring the Revolution to a successful close, he used to print off little stories on his private press at Passy, just outside Paris. One of those stories recounted a remarkable dream about Debby. He dreamt he went to heaven, "the Elysian Fields," and tried to reclaim her, "but she said to me: 'I have been your good wife 49 years and 4 months, almost half a century. Be content with that.'"[16]

What's remarkable about that dream is he could not remember his own wedding anniversary. They had been married 44, not 49, years. To Debby it must have seemed much longer, but she "had taken up a resolution never to make any complaint to you or give you any disquiet —"[17] and she kept that promise to the very end.

Extracts from Deborah Franklin's Letters

> Commander of British forces in America, John Campbell, Lord Loudon, transmitted a complaint about the post office at Philadelphia charging postage for official, franked letters. His order, now at the Huntington Library (LO 5366), dated 9 January 1758, threatened to haul the deputy postmaster before the House of Lords for such contemptuous behavior. Acting for her absent husband, Mrs. Franklin tried to excuse his deputy who also happened to be her niece's husband, William Dunlap, and then offered a complaint of her own:

Honoured Sir:

I understand there have been Complaints made to you against the Deputy Post-Master in this Town. I am sorry if there be any Grounds for them; but in Justice to the Young Man who is a Relation of Mr. Franklin's, I must say if any Wrong is done, it is not to be charged upon him. He took money for no Letters but what came charged to him from other Officers, nay even in that Case from none of the Officers, who made any Scruple about paying him. Besides as he is but lately come into the Office, he might not know that your Lordship's Name upon a Letter gave it a Frank. I cannot therefore help thinking that the charging him with wrongfully exacting sounds very harsh.

I am not fond of complaining otherwise I might have before informed you, that I think I have been treated very unpolitely. I might say insulted in my own House by Sir John Sinclair in an Affair of this Nature. I will not trouble your Lordship with particulars, but only say if the Complaints made against the Post-Office here came from him they are very unjust. —

Now I have taken the freedom to write to your Lordship, allow me to say that Mr. Franklin has at a considerable expence set up two Riders to carry Intelligence regularly twice a Week between this Town and New York. But of late under Colour of your Lordship's Name they have been so detained at New-York, that the Days of their coming in and setting out are quite altered, and sometimes we have Intelligence but once a Week, which the Merchants here complain of as a considerable Disappointment.

I would just mention one thing more: that since Mr. Franklin went abroad, I have given particular Orders that no Express on His Majesty's Service be detained in the Post-Office above three Hours, and if the post was not ready to set out, a Man and Horse have been hired immediately to carry it. This has been expensive, and is like to be more so, as the Riders are detained. — I therefore hope your Lordship will order the Posts for the future to be regularly discharged from New-York; and I shall be glad to know how the Charges of Expresses may be defrayed.

Philadelphia, 20 January 1758 [Huntington Manuscript LO 5425]

[The letter to Lord Loudon was probably written from her dictation by a clerk. Mrs. Franklin's own handwriting seems sometimes undecipherable, made doubly difficult because she spelled words as she pronounced them; e.g. speaking of a letter just received, "hough am I plesed to reed over and over a gen I Cole it a husbands Love Letter." I have therefore modernized passages from her letters, extracted from volumes 12- 17 of *Papers of Benjamin Franklin*, with volume and page references in parentheses. These were written to her husband during the years, 1765-1774, he was serving as colonial agent, or lobbyist, in London. She addressed him as "My dear Child" or, less often, "My dear Benny."]

February 1765

I am set down to confab a little with my dear child as it seems a sort of a holiday, for we have an ox roasting on the river, and most people seems pleased with the affair, but as I partake of none of the diversions I stay at home and flatter myself that the next packet [boat] will bring me a letter from you. (12:43)

April 1765

April 7. This day is complete five months since you left your own house. I did receive a letter from the Capes; since that, not one line. I do suppose that you did write by the January packet, but that is not arrived as yet. Miss Wikoff came and told me that you was arrived and was well, that her Brother had wrote her that he had seen you. Mr. Neate has wrote that you was well, and Miss Graham has wrote that you was well. All these accounts are as pleasing as such things can be, but a letter would tell me how your poor arm was and how you was on your voyage, and how you are, and every thing is with you — which I want very much to know. (12:101)

October 1765

October 6. O my Child there is great odds between a man's being at home and abroad, as everybody is afraid they shall do wrong, so everything is left undone. (12:298)

October 8. I have been so happy as to receive several of your dear letters within these few days and to see a man that had seen you. He tells me you look well, which is next to seeing of you. How am I pleased to read over and over again — I call it a *husband's Love letter.* . . . I have wrote several letters to you, one almost every day, but then I could not forbear saying something to you about public affairs. Then I would destroy it, and then begin again, and burn it again, and so on — but now I don't think to say one word about them as I believe you have it much better than I could tell you. (12:300)

January 1766

January 12. I have paid towards the land — I believe it is in Nova Scotia or some such place, but to be short, I have paid 53 pounds to young Wayne before the deeds is done, but he had borrowed the money of a man that was agoing out of town — so you see I am a real Land Jobber. I tell Sally this is for Grandchildren. She seemed very well pleased at it, and thinks we shall have some in good time. I hope I have done as you would have me or as you would if you had been at home yourself. (12:32)

May 1767

May 16. [Reporting a visit to Governor William, "Billy," Franklin at Burlington, New Jersey]. Billy come down with me on Monday and returned yesterday, and Sally went up with him and I expect her down this day or tomorrow. I was the readier to let her go as she is not very well and looks very pale so as to give me much uneasiness. But she always looks ill in summer, and two or three days changes her. But I think she has been made uneasy about her Brother who was challenged on Monday night. I should not have said one word to you but I think somebody will tell.

The Challenge was sent by young Hicks, brought by young Dr. Kearsley, very much in drink. Sally was very much scared and would not let her Brother go without her. So you see this daughter of ours is a mere Champion and thinks she is to take care of us. Her Brother and she is very happy together indeed, but I long to see her back again as I could not live above another day without her, as I am circumstanced — a mind sometimes fluttered, sometimes glad, then depressed and so on. O that you was at home! (14:1567-67)

October 1767

October 13. [On an intercolonial romance featuring 24-year-old Susanna Shippen and Reverend Samuel Blair of Boston's Old South Church, who subsequently turned down the offer to be President at Princeton; he was 26.] Now I am to tell you that our Sukey Shippen is married. It was a sort of runaway affair, although it is to a parson. He was called to Boston and settled there, and it had almost killed him and Sukey. So after a year he come back, and he appeared on a Saturday evening, on the Thursday after, she left her father's house and was married at her Aunt Willens and went to her husband's mother's and is returned to her father's again, but whether he has seen her, I can't say. But I am told that he is chosen President of Princeton College and is to be there in a year. But her father is so distressed about her leaving of him for that time that he won't let anybody say anything to him about it. I have been over to see Mrs. Shippen and comfort her as well as I can. (14:281-82)

January 1768

January 21-22. [Reporting on illness of her niece Deborah

Dunlap, whom she was nursing after a stroke.] The night before last, she was in great distress, calling on her uncle and said if he was there she should not be treated in such a manner. I sat by her and folded her in my arms, and told her that I would take as much care of her as though you was there, and held her for two hours and Sally sat at her feet and wrapped them up and had a thing to heat them a way. At least she fell asleep and was yesterday as happy as we could expect, and still continues more happy. I pray to God to continue it for her own sake as well as her children's. It is very hard on me, now more than 60 years old to be in every station. I am father and mother to our own, and so I must be to poor Debby by inclination and for credit sake. (15:24)

November 1769

November 20-27. [Commenting on recovering from stroke.] I am in hopes I shall get better again to see you. I often tell my friends I was not sick, I was only more to bear anymore, and so I fell down and could not get up again. Indeed it was not any sickness but too much disquiet of mind. But I had taken up a resolution never to make any complaint to you or give you any disquiet. About five or six days after I received your letter, Dr. Evens sent me his letter to let me know that you was well, for which I am thankfull. I have to tell you something of myself, what I believe you would not believe of me only I tell you myself. I have been to a play with Sister. I expect that somebody to speak to me, but I have been twice to the Presbyterian meeting, which will be worse to some folks. (16:231)

August 1770

August 16. I am very sorry to think I should not have it in my power to attend on you. When will it be in your power to come home? How I long to see you, but I would not say one word that would give you one moment's trouble. (17:205)

October 1770

October 14. It wants but a very few days of six years since you left home, and then you thought it would be but seven months. . . . My dear child, I hope you will not stay longer than this fall. I must conclude, your affectionate wife D Franklin. (17:253, 255)

Martha Washington, from a portrait by Gilbert Stuart

MARTHA DANDRIDGE CUSTIS WASHINGTON

Born 2 June 1731, New Kent County, Virginia.

Died of severe bilious fever 22 May 1802, Mount Vernon.

Eldest of eight children born to merchant-planter John Dandridge and Frances Jones Dandridge.

Wed Daniel Parks Custis, 1749; widowed July 1757.

Wed George Washington 6 January 1759.

Four children in first marriage — two died in infancy; John [Jack] (1754-81) and Martha [Patsy] (1763-73).

Adopted John's two youngest — Eleanor Custis (1779-1852) and George Washington Parke Custis (1781-1857).

MARTHA DANDRIDGE CUSTIS WASHINGTON

In a dual letter bringing former favorite neighbor Sally Fairfax up to date after a quarter century's absence, George Washington announced the Washington family had taken up permanent residence at Mount Vernon.[1] Martha Washington, adding news of the old neighborhood and family, explained that she too had been "a kind of perambulator" during "eight or nine years of war, and during another eight years" as First Lady. She regretted every minute of it away

15

from home, but never complained.

Her present delight, in 1798, was "the tranquil employment of rural life" and especially looking after her teenaged
grandchildren Eleanor — Nelly — and George Washington
Parke Custis who was then at school in Annapolis. Martha
Washington was resolved that this was the "life with which
my days will close."

Born and bred in Tidewater Virginia as Martha
Dandridge, she had not even left Virginia till the Revolution
broke out and, after a year-and-a-half's absence from
General Washington, she braved snow drifts by sleigh to go
to him at Valley Forge that memorial winter of 'Seventy-
eight.[2] Nearly there, her husband met her and hoisting her
tiny figure behind him on Nelson the horse, took her to share
the famine of the troops.

They called her "Lady Washington" for her compassion
and grace but were just as impressed by such homely behavior
as using thorns to substitute for steel pins, or calling the wives
at camp and all around in for daily sewing bees, producing
socks and shirts or mending clothes for the troops.

Very sensitive to the troops' morale, she routinely visited
the sick and wounded, asking about their families, sometimes
joining in their prayers. She encouraged their forming a
band, assuring them of the pleasure she took in the sound of
the fifes and drums, preferring it to "any music that was ever
heard."[3]

This was not putting on an act but obviously deep compassion: "The poor soldiers are without sufficient clothing
and food, and many of them are barefooted. Oh, how my
heart pains for them!"[4] That is why, basket in hand, through
snow or slush, she would slog her way from hut to hut mother-
ing the men during that awful winter at Valley Forge.

Hers was compassion from bitter experience of her own.
At 18, eldest of eight in a middle-class family, she had married
Daniel Custis, one of Virginia's wealthiest men. Twenty
years older than she, Custis had in fact been her godfather.
Their affection was no less tender. After 8 years of happy
union, he died suddenly intestate leaving her with a boy of 5,
a girl of 3, and a hopelessly entangled estate to manage.

That estate, by today's standards worth about six million dollars,[5] was split three ways among the widow and the two children. As good a manager as George Washington was, it would take him twenty years to straighten out the books. They were wed a year-and-a-half after Custis died, the ceremony at her home 6 January 1759. Her dowry: 17,000 acres of plantation land.[6] They would make their home at his estate, Mount Vernon.

Washington became legal guardian of little Patsy and Jack, calling them not "my" or "Mrs. Washington's" but "the" children. This was to emphasize that they were financially independent. Ordering their presents for the first Christmas together, he told the merchant to keep the boy's account separate from the girl's, billing each account by itself.[7]

This does not mean a lack of love. On the contrary, the family could not have been happier for the first dozen years. Mrs. Washington's constant piece of jewelry was the locket containing a strand of her husband's unpowdered hair.[8] Up to his becoming president, she would call him "Papa" or refer to him as her "old man."[9] When he became president, she began referring to him as "the General." He always called her "Patsy."

His increasing engagement in public affairs eroded the Mount Vernon idyll. She would attend the festivities at Alexandria with him and enjoy the socializing that erupted when the legislature met, but as war came closer and his absences more distant, she had to take on more responsibility for managing the plantation.

This meant more than mere agriculture. From the start and through 41 years of marriage they provided the warm, living center for an extended family of Dandridges and Washingtons near and far. Somebody counted about 2000 guests homing in on them during those early years, increasing her responsibility.[10]

While Washington attacked farming with military precision, rotating crops, raising sheep then processing the wool, raising wheat and milling it, even applying time-and-motion studies to increase the productivity of the 200-plus slaves they called their "people," Mrs. Washington acted as overseer of the mansion, schooling the "people" in domestic arts, serving as their counselor and comforter.

A visitor described a typical morning session.[11] The chambermaid sat on one side with her knitting, "on the other side a little colored pet learning to sew," and an elderly woman cutting out the families' winter clothes, while the mistress directed them all, incessantly knitting alongside "several pair of nice colored stockings and gloves she had just finished."

Such idyllic scenes were eradicated by the war and personal tragedy. In 1777 seventeen-year-old Patsy died from epilepsy. It was her legacy that helped the Washingtons finally achieve financial independence — but at what a cost! To understand how deeply devastating that death could be, consider that when Mrs. Washington spent a night away from one of her babies, she could not sleep a wink: "If I at any time heard the dogs bark or a noise ... I thought there was a person sent for me."[12]

A measure of consolation came when eighteen-year-old Jacky married Nancy Calvert. Mrs. Washington, too grief-stricken to attend the ceremony, sent her new daughter-in-law a note:

"God took from me a daughter when June roses were blooming — He has now given me another daughter, to warm my heart again. I am as happy as one so afflicted and so blest can be."[13]

They blessed her further with four grandchildren, three girls and a boy, to help heal the hurt.

For a half-dozen years of the war, she had refused to allow Jacky to join the army. With her husband as commanding general, her word was law. Even when Jacky was an unwed lad and his mother had given permission to have him vaccinated, her husband had it done secretly to spare her the terror he knew she would feel.

This is not to say that she lacked courage in other matters. In Fall 1775 the British were threatening to attack the region around Mount Vernon. Neighbor George Mason sent his family "many miles back in the country, and advised Mrs. Washington to do likewise."[14] She at first refused, "No, I will not desert my post." Then reluctantly rode back a few miles. But the "plucky little woman," reported Mason, "stayed away only one night."

Her desire to keep Jacky from the front seemed more deep-seated. With the victory at Yorktown she finally relented, succumbing to his incessant pleas. General Washington appointed him an aide to family friend La-Fayette — only to have poor Jacky Custis cut down at Yorktown by camp fever. Together the Washingtons sped to his bedside, arriving only in time to see him "breathe his last."[15] The attending physician had to minister to the collapsed parents, paralyzed with grief.

The young Nancy Calvert Custis had plenty of family connections of her own. Still the Washingtons relieved some of her burden and much of their grief by adopting her two youngest children, two-and-a-half year-old Nelly and six-months-old Washington.

As the war wound down and Washington sought retirement, Mount Vernon became a shrine for visitors from all over the Western world. While Washington went off to look after his lands in the West, the entertaining was left to Mrs. Washington. In fact, it took at least a year for them to finally have dinner together alone.[16]

One family legend tells how a gaggle of nieces came in to dine in their casual dresses, a clear violation of house rules.[17] Mrs. Washington said nothing during the meal. The girls sat dawdling at the table. Then one of them saw a carriage-full of young officers, Washington's aides, coming up the drive. The girls begged to be excused to dress properly. Mrs. Washington said, "No. Stay as you are! What's good enough for General Washington is good enough for any guest."

Visitors from abroad especially were not used to seeing a lady of her station in life dressed in homespun, working at her spinning wheel or moving expertly among carpenters, bricklayers, bakers, even grocers who operated her "people's" own store. To help her manage this self-sufficient society, her niece Fanny came to live with the Washingtons, soon marrying a nephew of the General — another George Washington — so Mount Vernon stayed in good hands when the call came to inaugurate a president.

Mrs. Washington expected that call. Her husband had presided over the convention that proposed the federal constitution in the summer of 1787. Delegates then said that they had Washington in mind as they drafted the unprecedented office of president.[18] The first presidential election unanimous in his favor left no doubt that he would make the sacrifice.

Both Washingtons would have preferred to stay home. The first and dearest wish of her heart, said Mrs. Washington, was that they should have been allowed to grow old together at Mount Vernon. But she knew the price of patriotism: "I cannot blame him for having acted according to his ideas of duty."[19]

And even amidst the frothy life as First Lady she accepted her own role as duty. "When I was younger I should probably have enjoyed the innocent gayeties of life as much as most persons of my age; but I had long since placed all the prospects of my future worldly happiness in the still enjoyments of the fireside at Mount Vernon."[20]

The role of First Lady, or "presidentess," required her to play two opposing parts — a majestic "Lady Washington" and a downhome next-door-neighbor woman not much different from any other woman in this great democracy of ours. The downhome role was second nature to her. The royal side of the role only seemed natural to her because she felt so awkward and shy that her manner appeared haughty and aloof — but never supercilious.

Her initial journey to the inaugural set the pattern. Washington had gone on ahead. She had her own triumphal procession northward — military escorts, throngs throwing flowers in her path. Between Philadelphia and Trenton the weather grew threatening, and she stopped the procession.[21] She asked that the military escort go home to shelter before she would proceed.

Martha Washington knew that as First Lady everything she did set a precedent for future First Ladies, so she tried to do everything properly. Aides to the President who had served in foreign embassies tried to coach her in etiquette of courts. This made sense since most Americans had grown up under George III and so expected their rulers to do as he had done.

One consequence for Mrs. Washington was discarding her comfortable homespun for imported silks, satins, velvet and lace. She had to replace downhome open house with Friday evening receptions — plumcake, tea and coffee — which she would close with the remark: "The General always retires at nine o'clock and I usually precede him."[22] These receptions were unfortunately scheduled from 8 to 10.

Besides those full-dress receptions, she also had to entertain at Wednesday dinners for congressmen, ambassadors, and selected guests. Sometimes she would have cabinet officers over to meet while drinking wine. Often she and her small group of friends, most notably Molly Morris, Sally Jay, and Abigail Adams, would take sightseeing excursions. That was pretty much the social life during eight years of the first presidency.

Having the grandchildren with her was a special treat but very expensive, especially considering that the President rejected a salary and tried to please Congress by keeping his expenses low. Yet Mrs. Washington confessed: "My grandchildren and domestic connections make up a great portion of the felicity which I looked for in this world. I shall hardly be able to find any substitute that would indemnify me for the loss."[23]

She was not complaining about those around her who tried to make her duty tolerable. "No," she said, "God forbid! for everybody and everything conspire to make me as contented as possible."[24] She told Betsy Hamilton that people must think the First Lady would be extremely happy. "They might more properly call me the Chief State Prisoner."[25] She just wanted to go home.

The next-best thing to going home was writing to her niece Fanny with advice on managing Mount Vernon and even on managing Fanny's infant children.[26] Advising on the baby's tummy aches: "I have not a doubt but worms is the principal cause of her complaints. Children that eat every thing as they like and feed as heartily as yours do must be full of worms —

"Indeed, my dear Fanny, I never saw children stuffed as yours was when I was down and rather wondered that they were able to be tolerable with such loads as they used to put into their little stomacks." And this was only her nieces' children, a kind of rehearsal for advising grand-daughter Nelly in years to come.

Shortly after the Washingtons returned to Mount Vernon for good, the General's nephew, Lawrence Lewis, came to help him manage the plantation. Lewis was child of Washington's favorite sister, and Nelly Custis was his favorite from infancy. The match was inevitable. They wed by candlelight on his birthday, 22 February 1799, and six months later Washington presented them with a part of the Mount Vernon tract.

A while after that, a visitor remarked how beautiful and charming Nelly behaved to "her aged Grandmother and the General, whom she always called Grand-pa."[27] She presented them with a baby great-grandaughter, Frances, two-and-a-half weeks before George Washington died.

He suffered throat problems from boyhood. Very early in the morning of December 12, 1799, he awoke Mrs. Washington with his difficult breathing. Though he could barely speak, he kept her from going for a servant, for that would have meant getting up in the cold. He died shortly after that pathetic scene. "I only wish," she said, "soon to follow him."[28] She kept to her room.

Once again a little child brought renewed energy. Baby Frances and her parents lived with grandmama two more years. Sighed Nelly, "My only fear is my daughter will be spoilt, she is indulged in everything, stays with grandmama the most part of every day and is never denied anything she takes a fancy to."[29]

Visitors seldom saw Widow Washington, for she kept to her own rooms. Those who were lucky enough to visit with her were amused by her old fashioned dress. She assured one young man that, though she did read the newspapers, she was no politician.[30] Having had a front row seat at the momentous scenes of the Revolution, she was now content to let history pass by the upstairs windows of Mount Vernon. She burnt Washington's letters to her and hers to him.

Death released her on May 22, 1802, with a bilious fever. In anticipation, she had sent a servant for the white night gown set aside for this last scene.[31] With toddler Frances and baby Martha strangely silent downstairs, she peacefully expired.

Nelly would go on to have eight children in all, only four living to maturity. But naturally when baby Frances grew up to have babies of her own and moved to Cincinnati, Nelly was not negligent in passing on the legacy once shared with cousin Fanny, the wit and wisdom of bringing up babies by the First Grandmother of the USA.

Extracts from Martha Washington's Letters

The first three samples reflect the unhappy life away from Mount Vernon, first at the front during the war, later as First Lady in New York. The others, to her favorite niece Fanny Washington, display a characteristic combination of maternal concern and mental toughness her position required. In Martha Washington's absence, Fanny looked after Mount Vernon's domestic affairs. Widowed with three children in February 1793, she wed Washington's secretary, Tobias Lear, a year and a half later, and died in March 1796.

January 1776

[To her favorite sister Nancy, from Cambridge, Massachusetts, 31 January 1776:] I have wrote to you several times, in hopes it would put you in mind of me, but I find it has not had its intended effect. I am really very uneasy at not hearing from you and have made all the excuses for you that I can think of, but it will not do much longer. If I do not get a letter by this night's post, I shall think myself quite forgot by all my friends. The distance is so long, yet the post comes in regularly every week.

The General, myself, and Jack are very well. Nelly Custis [Jack's wife] is, I hope, getting well again and, I believe, is with child. I hope no accident will happen to her in going back; I have not thought much about it yet. God knows where we shall be. I suppose there will be a change soon, but how, I can't pretend to say.

A few days ago, General [Sir Henry] Clinton and several companies sailed out of Boston Harbor, to what place destined for, we cannot find out. Some think to Virginia he is going, others to New York. They have been kept in Boston so long that I suppose they will be glad to seek for a place where they may have more room, as they cannot get out of the way here but by water.

Our navy has been very successful in taking their vessels. Two was taken last week loaded with coals and potatoes, wines and several other articles for the use of the troops. If

General Clinton is gone to New York, General Lee is there before him, and I hope will give him a warm reception. He was sent there some time ago to have matters put into proper order in case any disturbance should happen, as there are many Tories in that part of the world, or at least many are suspected to be very unfriendly to our cause at this time. . . . [*Historical Magazine*, 2 (May 1858) 134- 35]

November 1789

[To her Boston friend Mercy Otis Warren from New York probably November 26, talking about the Washingtons' response to the national outpouring of respect and confidence:] With respect to myself, I sometimes think the arrangement is not quite as it ought to have been, that I, who had much rather be at home, should occupy a place with which a great many younger and gayer women would be prodigiously pleased.

As my grandchildren and domestic connections made up a great portion of the felicity which I looked for in this world, I shall hardly be able to find any substitute that would indemnify me for the loss of such endearing society. I do not say this because I feel dissatisfied with my present station. No, God forbid! for everybody and everything conspire to make me as contented as possible in it. Yet I have learned too much of the vanity of human affairs to expect felicity from the splendid scenes of public life.

I am still determined to be cheerful and to be happy in whatever situation I may be, for I have also learned from experience that the greater part of our happiness or misery depends on our disposition and not upon our circumstances. We carry the seeds of the one or the other about with us in our minds wherever we go. [HM 18781]

October 1789

[To Fanny among directions for managing the Mount Vernon household in a letter dated 22 October:] Mrs. Sims will give you a better account of the fashions than I can. I live a very dull life here and know nothing that passes in the town — I never go to any public place — indeed I think I am more like a state prisoner than anything else, there is certain bounds set for me which I must not depart from — and as I cannot do as I like I am obstinate and stay at home a great deal. [A.H. Wharton, *Martha Washington* 205-206]

June 1794

[On child development, to Fanny 15 June from Philadelphia:] I am sorry to hear by your letter of the tenth that your little girl has been so ill — I hope she has got quite well before this. I have not a doubt but worms is the principle cause of her complaints. Children that eat everything as they like and feed as heartily as yours does must be full of worms. Indeed, my dear Fanny, I never saw children stuffed as yours when I was down and rather wondered that they were able to be tolerable with such loads as they used to put into their little stomachs. I am sure there is nothing so pernicious as overcharging the stomach of a child with every kind of food that they will take. Experience will convince you of the impropriety if nothing else will. [ed. W.K. Bixby, privately printed 1922]

September 1794

[Three months later, now from suburban Germantown in hopes of escaping yellow fever, Martha Washington addresses Fanny on the same topic:] I am sorry to hear by your letter of the tenth that Fayette has been sick. As you were giving him the bark, I hope he is now perfectly well. This is a season for children to have complaints of different kinds and as you let your children eat as much fruit or anything else as they will, I am not surprised that a delicate child like Fayette is sick, for certain it is that children should not eat everything that they will. Experience is the only thing that will convince a fond mother that her child should be in some instance controlled in their diet. I hope it will be soon that you will see it or that child will suffer very much in his health. . . .

I very sincerely wish you would exert yourself so as to keep all your matters in order yourself without depending upon others, as that is the only way to be happy — to have all your business in your own hands without trusting to others that will promise and perhaps never think of doing it till they see you. I would rouse myself and not trouble any mortal. Your concerns are not so large but you might with proper attention have them always kept in good order. I hope, my dear Fanny, you will look upon this advice in the friendly way it is meant, as I wish you to be as independent as your circumstances will admit, and to be so is to exert yourself in the management of your estate. If you do not, no one else will. A dependence is, I think, a wretched state, and you have enough if you will manage it right. [HM 5066]

September 29. [Fanny has asked the Washingtons' advice on marrying the President's secretary Tobias Lear:] My dear Fanny, I wish I could give you unerring advice . . . . I really don't know what to say to you on the subject. You must be governed by your own judgment, and I trust Providence will direct you for the best. It is a matter more interesting to yourself than any other. The person contemplated is a worthy man and esteemed by everyone that is acquainted with him. He has, it is conceived, fair prospects before him . . . . As to the President, he never has nor never will, as you have often heard him say, intermeddle in matrimonial concerns. He joins me, however, in wishing you every happiness this world can give . . . . but no more than myself would not wish to influence your judgment either way — yours and the children's good being among the first wishes of my heart. [A. H. Wharton, *Martha Washington* 247-8]

October 19. Your happiness, my dear Fanny, is, I assure you, very dear to the President and myself. I have no doubt but you have considered well what you are about to undertake, and I hope that the same Providence that has hitherto taken care of you will still be your guardian angel to protect and direct you in all your undertakings. You have my fervent prayers for your happiness. [ibid 250]

November 30 The President seemed a good deal surprised at the quantity of wine that you have given out, as it never was his intention to give wine or go to any expence to entertain people that came to Mount Vernon out of curiosity to see the place. If it is continued, we shall have but very little for ourselves if we should come home. Rum may always be had. And I beg you will not give another bottle out of the vault (cellar). I make not the least doubt that Frank (the servant) drinks as much wine as he gives to the visitors — and rum both — and wish you not to give more out unless the President should order it. [HM 5068]

Spring 1797

[Although John Rodehamel, former Mount Vernon expert, reports this letter spurious, I include this excerpt because it has been so widely quoted:] I cannot tell you, my dear friend, how much I enjoy *home* after having been deprived of one so long, for our dwelling in New York and Philadelphia was not *home*, only sojourning. The General and I feel like children just released from school or from a hard taskmaster, and we believe that nothing can tempt us to leave the sacred roof tree again, except on private business or pleasure. . . .

Our furniture and other things sent us from Philadelphia arrived safely, our plate we brought with us in the carriage. How many dear friends I have left behind! They fill my memory with sweet thoughts. Shall I ever see them again? Not likely unless they shall come to me here, for the twilight is gathering around our lives. I am again fairly settled down to the pleasant duties of an old-fashioned Virginia housekeeper, steady as a clock, busy as a bee, and cheerful as a cricket. [A.H. Wharton, *Martha Washington* 264-5]

May 1798

[This succinct summary was for ex-next-door neighbor Sally Fairfax who since the outbreak of the war had been living in England. The letter from Mount Vernon is dated 17 May:]

It is among my greatest regrets, now I am again fixed (I hope for life) at this place, at not having you as a neighbor and companion. This loss was not sensibly felt by me while I was a kind of perambulator during eight or nine years of the war and during other eight years which I resided at the seat of the general government, occupied in scenes more busy, though not more happy, than in the tranquil employment of rural life with which my days will close.

The changes which have taken place in this country since you left it (and it is pretty much the case in all other parts of this State) are, in one word, total. In Alexandria, I do not believe there lives at this day a single family with whom you had the smallest acquaintance. . . .

With respect to my own family, it will not I presume be new to you to hear that my son died in the fall of 1781. He left four fine children, three daughters and a son; the two eldest of the former are married and have three children between them, all girls. . . . The youngest daughter, Eleanor, is yet single and lives with me, having done so from an infant, as has my grandson George Washington, now turned of seventeen, except when at college — to three of which he has been, viz., Philadelphia, New Jersey and Annapolis, at the last of which he now is. [W.C. Ford, *Writings of George Washington* 13:500-501]

Grace Galloway, painted from a drawing by Stokes

GRACE GROWDON GALLOWAY

Birthdate and place unknown — 1732, probably Trevose, Bucks County, Pennsylvania.

Died 6 February 1782 in Philadelphia.

Youngest of three daughters born to judge and wealthy land-owner Lawrence Growdon and first wife Elizabeth Nicholls Growdon.

Wed Joseph Galloway, 18 October 1753; abandoned June 1778.

Four children — three boys died in infancy; Elizabeth (about 1757-1815).

Kept detailed diary 17 June 1778 - 30 September 1779.

GRACE GROWDON GALLOWAY

The summer of 1778 found Philadelphia in turmoil. After occupying the city for a year the British troops pulled out, taking with them any loyalists who wished to leave. Patriots who had spent the year exiled to rural Lancaster came back to punish collaborators who had remained. Those were chiefly pacifist Quakers who had stayed in the city taking care of business. They now risked losing all they owned through confiscation. Worst off were the wives of those who fled with the British leaving families destitute and soon to become homeless and exiled.

The leading figure among these abandoned wives was Grace Growdon Galloway, except that she was not abandoned but rather had insisted on remaining behind when her husband and her only daughter left with the British. Her husband had been the long-term speaker of the state legislature during the turbulent years leading to the Revolution. He had served the British occupation as chief civil administrator — chief of both police and the port. She was therefore the first target for confiscation agents.

Her reasoning in remaining behind was legalistic. The Galloways' extensive real estate holdings had come to her from her father, and a pre-marriage contract gave Galloway use of the lands but not ownership. In remaining behind she was preserving and protecting her property for their daughter Betsy, to prevent her having to go through what her mother was now suffering.

During the previous year and even during the many years of Galloway's public service for the colony she had floated above politics, a *grand dame* even in her middle age, ruling majestically over the ancestral estate, Trevose, in lush Bucks County bordering Philadelphia. She played lady bountiful: One of her husband's law students about to drop out and turn actor because his mother would no longer support him was rescued by Mrs. Galloway's offer to support him until he could support himself.[1]

She was Bucks County's "great folks." She and Betsy would ride out in their elegant coach-and-four to visit a select handful of neighbors — Collisons, Kirkbrides, Richardsons — but only once a year per family in a perennial ritual marked by sheer elegance: "They would stay and take tea; the horses must not be taken from the coach but stand before the door, and the driver stand by and mind them until they were ready to go home."[2]

This was the imperial presence confronting the confiscation agents. Their leader was painter Charles Willson Peale, homegrown patriot just returned from arduous service with frontline troops and keenly aware of Philadelphia's lukewarm support for the war effort. Responsible for confiscating and selling loyalists' property, he would have to use all his skill in engaging popular support for what he acknowledged was a distasteful job; but somebody had to do it.[3] Then, besides her husband's notoriety, Grace Galloway represented the closest thing to American aristocracy and elegant respectability.

Given that kind of popular image, Grace Galloway, now 45 and residing in her elegant townhouse on Market Street, seemed the ideal role model for Peale's purposes. It helped that her house was next door to the headquarters of Benedict Arnold, at that time the military governor of Philadelphia for the patriots and therefore the focus of regional attention. But Peale underestimated Grace Galloway.

Ten times he visited trying to negotiate a compromise. She finally agreed to leave the house if Peale would promise not to confiscate it but only to rent it at a nominal sum. Just as the agreement came to signing, however, she found that one of Peale's agents had already rented the house without her knowledge. She dug in her heels.

They gave her a day's notice, only to find next day she had barred all doors and windows so that if the agents wanted the house they could take it only by forcing an entry. Peale turned to the attorney-general and then the ruling executive council for advice. All concurred that the agents should use any force necessary to dislodge her — since now more than one mere mansion was at issue. The authority of the new state was under siege, as seen from Peale's report and Mrs. Galloway's diary.[4]

Peale's report says that the agents broke their way in through the kitchen door only to find her standing there with one of her lawyers who gave them a written notice that they would be sued for breaking and entering unlawfully. Peale said, "They were willing to abide by the Consequences, as they had not acted without advice" of their own.

Mrs. Galloway's version of the event adds details. "A little after 10 oclock they knocked violently at the door three times. The third time I sent Nurse and called out myself to tell them I was in possession of my own House and would keep so, and that they should gain no admittance. Hereupon they went round in the yard and tried every door but could none open. Then they went to the Kitchen door and with a scrubbing brush which they broke to pieces they forced that open."[5] And there she faced them with her Philadelphia lawyer and a legal document.

Mrs. Galloway's diary adds that Peale read the document then "said he had studied the Law and knew they did right." She assured them, "Nothing but Force should get me out of my House."

They started by throwing her furniture into the street, reminding her that her husband had been much harsher on patriots during his administration. They then went over the house for hidden items to make sure she did not carry away anything of value. When Peale offered to send next door to borrow General Arnold's carriage, "I told him he need not give himself the Trouble, for if I wanted the Chariot I could send to the General myself."

Peale did, however, send for the carriage discreetly. The general's housekeeper came over to let her know Arnold had placed a carriage at her disposal. "I then," she said, "accepted of it." Peale reports that he then took her "by the hand and conducted Mrs. Galloway to the chariot." Her version says more:

"Peel said the Chariot was ready but he would not hasten me. I told him I was at home in My own House and nothing but force should drive me out of it. He said it was not the first time he had taken a Lady by the Hand. An insolent wretch.

"This speech was made sometime in the room. At last he beckoned for the Chariot, for the General would not let it come till I wanted it. And as the Chariot drew up, Peel fetched my Bonnets and gave one to me . . . and with greatest air said, 'Come, Mrs. Galloway, give me your hand.'

"I answered, 'Indeed I will not nor will I go out of my house but by force.'

"He then took hold of my arm and I rose and he took me to the door. I then took hold on one side and looked round and said, 'Pray, take notice I do not leave my house of my own accord or with my own inclination but by force and nothing but force should have made me give up possession.'

"Peel said with a sneer, 'Very well, Madam,' — and when he led me down the step I said, 'Now Mr. Peel, let go my Arm. I want not your assistance.'

"He said he could help me to the Carriage. I told him I could go without, 'And you, Mr. Peel, are the last Man on earth I would wish to be obliged to—'" Clearly she was setting him up to be sued for "forcible entry" with a Philadelphia lawyer by her side throughout the scene.

Yet Peale's plan worked. Seeing Grace Galloway evicted made others more pliable. She herself saw the results. Becky Shoemaker lived just across Market Street. Her husband too had fled with the British. He had been Joseph Galloway's partner in the civil administration of the city. Now, "Becky Shoemaker has agreed to go out of her House quietly" — and Grace Galloway found herself a notorious trouble-maker, "made the butt of" though Quakers were making a heroine out of Becky. And when Mrs. Galloway tried to sue for forced entry, "No one would join me," she said.

Becky Shoemaker avoided her, not wishing "to be looked on as her friend." Half self-pitying, half proudly, Mrs. Galloway remarked, "I belong to Nobody." Almost as proof of this, she would accept hospitality for only brief periods until after three months of seldom sleeping in the same bed twice, she consented to live with Deborah Morris, well known for looking after the homeless, one of Mrs. Galloway's friends from her first coming to Philadelphia as a 21-year-old bride.

As Grace Growdon, she had lived her early teen years with married sister Elizabeth in England where educational opportunities were superior. Their father, however, made her come home when he heard she planned to elope with the son of the local customs collector. Her marriage to Joseph Galloway seemed more promising since he was then an ambitious, rising young lawyer with a brilliant political future. The intimacy of their union may be gathered from the fact that within a couple of weeks after the ceremony, he had ridden off to travel the judicial circuit.

Mrs. Galloway seemed more amused than mournful. She wrote humorous letters to sister Elizabeth describing local customs. She told about the wedding reception lasting a whole week: "All the gentlemen of your or your husband's acquaintance comes every day, between 11 and 12, to pay their compliments and drink punch. And just before they go away, the bridegroom comes for the bride and leads her down and introduces her to the whole company. And after everyone has [kissed] her, they set a little while, then drink her health and take their leave.

"But nothing in nature can be more confounding than to be dragged into the company of 12 or 16 men in a morning just to be kissed and stared at, and sometimes nobody but yourself and never no women but your bridesmaids — and I had but one — sometimes none. I think during the whole time I had upwards of 70 men to do me the honor of a kiss, which I would have given the world to be excused from."[6]

She received the womenfolk in a different fashion, staying at home to receive them for another month, "obliged to set up in a white satin nightgown and in the greatest form during the whole time" while a bridesmaid hands out "large pieces of cake in white paper." She sits through this "ceremonious farce" for a whole month before she can start returning visits, the sort of visits she would later make accompanied by daughter Betsy.

The Galloways had two other children, two boys who died as infants in 1755 and 1760. Elizabeth's birth was not in Quaker records but she was about 15 or 16 when in 1773 she replayed an episode from her mother's youth. Gossips reported Galloway had found Betsy about to elope with a scoundrel named Griffen (probably Samuel Griffen, later adjutant-general of Philadelphia militia during the war).[7] The irate parent took a shot at Griffen but missed. A half-dozen years later, Grace Galloway was still having nightmares about that scoundrel Griffen stealing her beloved Betsy, even though by that time Betsy was safe from his grasp and settled in England.

Mrs. Galloway began keeping a diary as a means of talking with her daughter, for in war, letters were slow and insecure. It took her almost six months after her husband and Betsy had left New York to find they had arrived safely in

England. They could be sure of security only if they sent letters through some secret conveyance. They sent her one wrapped in the lining of a pocketbook. And when secret couriers dared open letters to see if there were something they could do for her on this side of the Atlantic, Mrs. Galloway reacted, beginning her next letter to Betsy, "I wish the noble minded Heros on both Sides would let us women write without inspecting our scrawls."[8]

The diary represented her private feelings. "My dear child came into my mind and what she would say to see her Mamma walking five squares in the rain at Night like a common Woman and go to rooms in an Alley for her home I dare not think."[9] Sometimes the letters seem meant for prying eyes, as when Mrs. Galloway warns about changes in America where all ranks of the public have been affected by the war — "Truth and simplicity are fled to their native skies."

To Galloway himself she bluntly tells the truth. Her losses, she says, were "greater than any woman in the State" and "Few men could have supported what I have gone through nor bore as many indignities with that Fortitude that I have hitherto bore it."[10] Her body may be weakening, she adds, and this "has so weakened my mind that I fear I cannot support my Spirits to the last." Yet he must know the facts before she succumbs. She thereupon rehearsed the indignities she suffered from Peale and then her sometimes friends — subjected to pity "by the world which never gives it till a person is reduced and then they give it by way of Insult."

"I think it cannot be deemed vanity in a woman to say she has fortitude when the Facts are fairly stated," she said. But praise is not her aim. She perseveres in preserving her property so that beloved Betsy will never be subjected to what she herself has gone through. For that reason, though she lives only to see her again, she urges Galloway to keep their child on the English side of the Atlantic and would suffer anything rather than "see her here in a station different from that she has always been in."

More indignities were yet to come. With the surrender

of the British at Yorktown, the Quakers once again felt the fury of patriot mobs, this time for failing to light up their windows in celebration. Neighbor Becky Shoemaker had gone to join her husband in exile at New York, still in British hands, but her daughter Anna wrote her about the rioting in the old neighborhood:[11] "For two hours we had the disagreeable noise of stones banging about, glass crashing, and the tumultuous voices" until every house had a light in the windows. "A neighbour of ours had the effrontery to tell Mrs. Galloway that he was sorry for her furniture, but not for her windows."

Mrs. Galloway defied the law banishing wives of traitors. Unknown to her, her neighbors pleaded successfully that she had become too ill to travel. Those neighbors, however, also felt her defiance: "I told them I was the happiest Woman in Town for I had been stripped and turned out of doors yet I was still the same and must be Joseph Galloway's Wife and Lawrence Growdon's Daughter, and that it was not in their power to humble me for I should be Grace Growdon Galloway to the last."[12] And so she was.

She would copy out light verse railing against marriage, as:

> Never get Tied to a Man
> For when you are once in a yoke
> 'Tis all a mere Joke
> Of seeing your Freedom again.[13]

And also serious verse like the lines about being "Dead to each pleasing thought, each Joy of Life/ Turn'd to that heavy lifeless lump a Wife." Her diary entries echo that strain: "I despise and abhor his vanity and baseness .... Were it not for my dearest Child, I would embrace Poverty much sooner than live with a Man who would grasp at all I have yet treat me worse than a slave."

Yet on her deathbed, she called for Galloway: "I loved him and he me. Where is he? He don't know how ill I am or he would be with me."[14] Then, reported Deborah Morris, "She departed in a sweet easy manner much resigned" the sixth of February 1782.

It took the Pennsylvania Supreme Court another dozen years to rule that Grace Growdon Galloway had had the law on her side all along.[15] The property she had inherited from her father, Lawrence Growdon, subsequently passed on to Betsy. Betsy had once again replayed events in her mother's life, for remaining in England she had made a bad marriage with a young lawyer. The difference was that she could buy him off after a year, giving him £2000 pounds for sole custody of their baby girl, Grace Ann.[16] She too had made him sign a prenuptial contract, though not legal in Britain, giving up any claim to the property she inherited.

And so when Grace Ann came of age she came into her grandmother's inheritance. She subsequently split it up among her six children. Since she had married into the Irish aristocracy,[17] she did not wish to live in America nor did her children and they thus scattered the legacy that Grace Growdon Galloway had suffered so hard to preserve and protect for her daughter.

Extracts from Grace Growdon's Diary and Correspondence

Excerpts from the diary dating from June 1778 to July 1779 are drawn from the *Pennsylvania Magazine of History and Biography* 55(1931) 55-85 and from July 1779 to September 1779 from volume 58(1934) 152-89; excerpts from letters are from manuscripts in the Huntington Library.

Extract of Letter to Sister 1753

November 6. Tis so long since I took pen in hand that I am quite at a loss how to write — and even to you. But as I think it's absolutely necessary to write, if it's but nonsense, know then that the mighty change is come — and in plain terms, I am married.

The ceremony was performed the eighteenth of October at my papa's house in his parlor by one Rev. Peters, a very good and noted gentleman who has long since left off preaching, but he married us at my papa's request who he esteems as his particular friend. . . .

Mr. Galloway is now at Burlington Court, which is upwards of 20 miles from Philadelphia, and I am now left a few days quite alone in morning and evening. But as for afternoons I seldom want company, it being a custom among people of fashion here to stay at home a whole month to receive visits from the ladies, and I am obliged to set up in a white satin night gown and in the greatest form during the whole time.

And Polly Pennington, who was the only girl at the wedding, constantly attends to make tea and entertain the company, and after tea to put up large pieces of cake in white paper, which is handed to every lady after tea. When this ceremonious farce will be over, I scarecely know, but think I must set up one week longer, and then by the laws of politeness I may return my acquaintance visits. [HM 36845]

Diary Excerpts 1778

September 4. My dearest child sailed for England either the 17th or 18th.

September 25. I dreamed that the vessel in which Mr. G and my child sailed in was sunk and that they were all lost. I thought I would not believe it till Tommy Eddy told me it was not true, but that there was five or six men of war taken or lost. I then thought the news true and awoke in fright. I went to sleep again and dreamed my dear child was going home with me to Trevose and that it rained and she was but poorly and by the coachman's not driving right we were obliged to walk to the carriage and the road was full of water and she got wet in her feet and I was greatly distressed, but a poor fellow took her up to carry her to the carriage, but I was afraid she had taken her death before. We was afterward plagued about the carriage and drove into a narrow place and was in great danger. I awoke in terror.

November 25. Want to write to my dearest child but cannot. Have such dreadful thoughts of her being dead that I have no peace and am determined to go to her in the spring. As to myself, I am more agreeable than any time I ever spent since I married, but my child is dearer to me than all nature, and if she is not happy or anything should happen to her, I am lost. Indeed, I have no other wish in life than her welfare, and indeed I am concerned for her father but his unkind treatment makes me easy — nay, happy — not to be with him. And if he is safe, I want not to be kept so like a slave as he always made me in preventing every wish of my heart.

November 27. If J G's eyes are not yet opened to those he calls his friends, he is then unworthy of my attention, but his baseness has pulled down me and my child with him. Every insolence I meet with from these low fellows makes me reflect on the treatment I have met with on their account, and the little care he has taken to keep me from being insulted by them.

December 6. I was in so merry a humor that I cannot account for it — did nothing but laugh and sing to myself the whole day.

December 10. I was not well but building castles in the air drives my child from my thoughts or I must be more unhappy. At present am easy.

December 16. This unhappy man has ruined himself and

I find he conceals all he can for me. Was it not for my child I would never care anything about him, for his base conduct to me when present and his taking no care of me in his absence has quite made me indifferent to him.

Diary Excerpts 1779

March 7. Heard J G and my dear child were arrived in London, my dearest child was well, and that there is a letter for me at New York. I am very glad of this news but am impatient for my letter and fearful what situation they are in.

March 30. Got the letters from my dear child and her father. Am glad to hear they are well but no way satisfied as to their way of life.

May 4. Got up this morning and about 9 oclock received two letters from my dear child and two from her father in a pocketbook. I am now more easy as I hope from what they write we shall not sink and they are well and happy.

May 15. Was very low at night but sat and wrote a letter to my child between 12 and 1 oclock — am something easier.

Extract, Letter May 15

My mind is now so relieved on account of your health and welfare that it has little more to wish but to be with you. I tremble lest you should venture here. Had you not liked England I should have been completely wretched, for know, my dear, war with its iron hand corrupts the manners and invades the mind as much as it destroys the body, and all ranks of people are more or less affected by it.

Truth and simplicity are fled to their native skies. In short, America is not the same. The very element seems changed. Nor do I wish to see my child on this side of the Atlantic. If your Papa must return, I beg you will stay with your aunt and make no more voyages. This would be my advice to your Papa also for reasons I must not now give but I must leave it to your selves to pray God to direct you right.

I am not pleased with this scribble, but when my mind is under restraint I cannot either talk or write well. I have not now said what I want to say — oh, that I could give a scope to my imagination. My heart is full and my ideas flow rapid, but

I must restrain them and write for make nothings.

I sent this letter. It was returned, but it will now get to the Shoemakers safe. Since this was wrote I received your kind present of the pocketbook which I value on your account. Your letters I can answer in no other way but to tell you, wishing I could take you in my arms and assure you that you have one friend that will never forget you one moment and whose happiness is inseparable from your own.

Let me know how I must proceed. I long to see my sister and relations. Nothing else is worth my notice. Be polite to all but intimate with none. An easy deportment is the best recommendation. Do that which is just and right and leave the rest. Neither be arrogant nor servile — both are the mark of a mean mind. Yours wants not much cultivation. Adieu, my dear child. -G G

[The letter continues, now addressed to husband Joseph, to whom she complains that her losses have been greater than those of any woman in the state:] Few men could have supported what I have gone through nor bore the many indignities I have received with that fortitude that I had hitherto bore it. But the state of my body has so weakened my mind that I fear I cannot support my spirits to the last. I think it cannot be deemed vanity in a woman to say she has fortitude when the facts are fairly stated. See then a short account:

I have been taken by the arm and led out of my own house, all my inheritance taken from me, my father's house in the country in possession of strangers, left without friends or relations to take me in, pitied by the world which never gives in till a person is reduced and they give it by way of insult. 'Tis as much to say, "Now you are below my envy." . . . As to mortifications, I have got over them. [HM 36846]

Diary Excerpts 1779, continued

[Having ripped the lining of the pocketbook sent May 4, she finds two more letters secreted there:]

May 20. That was far from a balm. They were a dagger to my mind, as I find my child is *not* happy.

June 17. I sat in my room till 5 oclock reading the Arabian

Nights Entertainment but my whole heart was taken up with my child, and I traced in my mind the whole of that dreadful day in which I last saw her. I was going out but recollected this day twelvemonth and would not go out. Am greatly distressed as I see no more prospect of meeting them again than I did ten months past. [Fearing she will never see daughter Elizabeth again, this diary will explain her motives in remaining apart — so as not to abandon hope of retaining the estate.]

August 27. As to J G, though I have some affection for him, yet I despise and abhor his vanity and baseness and am now truly set against him. Yet I do not tell anyone. This makes it worse to bear. But all his unkindness is in my mind, and all within stress and confusion. It seems quite an outcast of mankind and my soul struck with a thousand daggers to find how this man has imposed upon me as well as treated me unkindly. Was it not for my dearest child, I would embrace poverty much sooner than live with a man who would grasp at all I have, yet treat me worse than a slave. And I fear my child will feel his ill humor . . . . but I will never live with him more.

Excerpt from Letter of Deborah Morris to Joseph Galloway 1782

May 29. [Reporting Mrs. Galloway's death, Mrs. Morris recapitulates her life since Galloway left then describes her dying:] On the sixth of the second month [February] last, she departed in a sweet, easy manner much resigned and composed after having her desire granted — mercifully granted by an evident confirmation of her hope in eternal happiness. She then laid in a sweet sleep for some time, and though I sat close by her, I could but just perceive her last breath.

There were present such as she desired should attend her last moments. Owen Jones and wife and daughter, Sukey, George Dilwyn who proved a most acceptable visitor, Mary Craig and her sister Peggy thy cousins, Ann Emlen, Hetty Fisher, my sister, self, Nourse, and my Rachel. . . . About an hour before her departure, she said, "I loved him and he me. Where is he? He don't know how ill I am or he would be with me soon." Except such little failures in memory, she was sensible to the last.

[Mrs. Morris goes on to assure Galloway that his late wife had been looked after by friends, including Dr. Jones who "had a great weight with those in power and obtained her release from banishment" — the punishment other Loyalist wives had suffered.] [HM 36871]

Abigail Adams, from the painting by Gilbert Stuart

ABIGAIL SMITH ADAMS

Born Weymouth, Massachusetts, 11 November 1744.

Died Quincy (formerly Braintree), Massachusetts, 28 October 1818 of typhoid fever.

Second of four children, three girls and a boy, born to Rev. William Smith and Elizabeth Quincy Smith.

Wed John Adams, 25 October 1764.

Five children — Abigail (1765-1813), Caroline (1795-1852), John Quincy (1767-1848), Charles (1770-1800), Thomas (1772-1832).

Joined husband at diplomatic posts in Europe May 1784-June 1788.

ABIGAIL SMITH ADAMS

The courtship of John Adams and Abigail Smith was carried on mostly by mail and consisted chiefly of much teasing back and forth, with a good deal of self-mockery on both sides. She kept teasing him to come up with a list of her faults so she could bring herself up to his standards. He sent a list of a half-dozen including "sitting with legs crossed."[1] He warned that this practice ruined the figure, injured the health, and signified "too much thinking."

She replied, concurring on most of the faults but demurring on the leg-crossing. "I think that a gentleman has no business to concern himself about the legs of a lady."[2] This was the kind of good-humored banter than would mark their 54 years of marriage surmounting the suffering of war, pestilence, and especially enforced absences for public service they both recognized would never be rewarded as the sacrifice deserved.

Abigail Adams assumed roles of both father and mother at the same time that she was expected to play roles of diplomat's wife, then first Second Lady and second First Lady. She happily abandoned the glitz and glamour of those roles to resume the basic role she felt assigned her by nature, just plain mother. Too late? Her children had children of their own, ample compensation for those 25 years of dizzy busyness.

In the Massachusetts of her youth, when preachers came close to constituting an aristocracy, she had been a preacher's daughter and the daughter of a mother born a Quincy, among the leading families of the region. John Adams came from a family of lower caste. Almost ten years older than she was, he was at first turned off by her "wit," gradually won over by her wit in another sense — native intelligence — for without formal schooling she was among the best-educated women in the land, tutored by her mother and father, nurtured by her father's library.

Their own household had only the library each could bring to it. For ten years their residence shifted from the farm in Braintree he had inherited to a succession of rented houses in Boston where he tried to build a law practice, most notoriously as counsel for British soldiers on trial for the Boston Massacre. More important were the children who came at two-year intervals during this period. The ensuing twenty-five years would see a continuing conflict in her duties as mother, wife, and patriot.

Alongside the natural functions of raising a family she considered educating them a moral obligation. Sometimes her reach in this respect exceeded society's grasp of what ladies particularly should know. John Adams had to warn 11-year-old Nabby to keep the lid on her ability to read the classics of antiquity in their original Greek and Latin — "It is scarcely respectable for young ladies to understand Latin and Greek."[3]

With experience Mrs. Adams herself was willing to adjust her reach, confiding to her sister that "Knowledge is a fine thing, and mother Eve thought so; but she smarted so severely for hers that most of her daughters have been afraid of it since."[4]

The sky was the limit with her sons. When somebody complained that 19-year-old Thomas was overstudying, she replied, "He who dies with studying dies in a good cause," for he will get to another world "much better calculated to improve his talents than if he had died a blockhead."[5]

But she grew convinced that womens' education should be utilitarian: "The finer accomplishments, such as music, dancing, and painting serve to set off and embellish the picture; but the groundwork must be formed of more durable colors" — those relating directly to "the useful and domestic duties of life,"[6]chiefly fulfilling the role of husband's helpmate. She was her own best model for that role.

On the eve of drafting the Declaration of Independence her husband received from her these ringing words: "Remember the ladies and be more generous and favourable to them than your ancestors. Do not put such unlimited power into the hands of the husbands."[7] Yet with the Revolution in force, she herself had to assume the unlimited power he abdicated in pursuit of public service's reward: fame. "These perilous times," she said, "swallow him up,"[8] leaving her to play the dual roles of mother and father, wife and husband.

Her primary duty, however, was as wife. She told her sister, "The all-wise Creator made woman an help-meet for man, and she who fails in these duties does not answer the end of her creation."[9] Nor was her role merely subservient. The biographies of great men, she said, show "some mother, or wife, or sister" behind their great deeds.[10] In fact, she assured her husband as the British moved to occupy Philadelphia, "A smart wife would have put General Howe in possession . . . a long time ago." She held these views long after John Adams retired: "No man," she wrote, "prospered in the world without the consent and cooperation of his wife."[11]

Her role as mother naturally had its demands, nursing the children through epidemics of smallpox, dysentery, and recurring fever, suffering herself stoically through a stillbirth and through death of a toddler. She took charge of their education as well as their inoculation, generally uncomplaining but every so often exploding — calling the absence of her husband at a time in the children's lives when they needed him most "one of the greatest misfortunes" of her own life.[12]

She most strongly felt the need of his "presence and advise" when tall, haughty daughter Nabby, in her early twenties, came close to marrying against her mother's wishes. Mrs. Adams investigated the boy's background thoroughly, interrogated him exhaustively, but still lacked confidence in her judgment. She took the easy way out by sailing across the Atlantic with Nabby to join Mr. Adams and the two elder sons he had with him in Europe.

This meant overcoming her fear of the ocean voyage and anxiety about taking care of business, but her concern over Nabby's potential elopement moved her more strongly. Ironically, a couple years later Nabby would marry William Smith in London. This former aide to Washington revealed himself to be a more dissolute person than the boy she left behind — Royal Tyler — who would go on to become America's premiere playwright.

But at least the move to Europe and England for a few years (1784-88) solved the problem of "a disorder call'd the Heartache," for which no "remedy [could] be found in America."[13] It also gave her a new perspective.

For almost ten years she had been wrapped up in buying farm stock, hiring help, looking after tenants, purchasing land, paying all bills, even establishing a little import business with the goods sent from her husband's posts in Europe.[14] She still managed to look after the farm by mail from overseas but the distractions of Continental social life were plenty.

Leaving England for home, she would tell Jefferson she preferred her farm to the Court of Saint James "where I seldom meet with characters so inoffensive as my hens and chickens or minds so well improved as my garden." Still, she enjoyed the pomp and ceremony and even the weird characters like Franklin's 65-year-old pal Madame Helvétius:

"The Doctor entered at one door, she at the other — upon which she ran forward to him, caught him by the hand, 'Hélas! Franklin,' then gave him a double kiss — one upon each cheek and another upon his forehead.

"When we went into the room to dine, she was placed between the Doctor and Mr. Adams. She carried on the chief of the conversation at dinner, frequently locking her hand into the Doctor's and sometimes spreading her arms upon the backs of both gentlemen's chairs, then throwing her arm carelessly upon the Doctor's neck . . . .

"After dinner she threw herself upon a settee, where she showed more than her feet. She had a little lap-dog who was, next to the Doctor, her favorite. This she kissed, and when he wet the floor, she wiped it up with her chemise."[15]

This kind of glamour and glitz did, however, impress Mrs. Adams, at least to the extent of conceding the need for a more pretentious place for the Adamses than the Braintree farm she had cultivated these many years. The next dozen years would see them shuttling back and forth between Braintree and national capitals in New York, then Philadelphia, and finally Washington. As first tenant of the brand new White House, still under construction — so damp each room needed fire going full time — she was ready to retire as plain old Abigail Adams.

Even her dedication as helpmeet could not force her to attend her husband's presidential inauguration. Nor could an avid insider's interest in politics, foreign or domestic, keep her any longer in the national capital than she had to be. As First Lady she had become a favorite target of the opposition press. They would call her Madam President or Mrs. President not of a nation but of a faction.[16] And she would take criticism of her husband as treason.

The paranoia that goes with the office of President seeped back to Braintree with her. Ten years earlier she could have used illness or death or "real laziness"[17] as excuses for not writing to one of her 500 correspondents. Now she stopped writing for two years, except to intimate family, for fear that her letters would be quoted out of context in the press. This was hardly the same Abigail Adams whose husband overseas urged her to tone down the intimacy of her letters for fear the enemy would intercept them and mock her.[18] She then could not care less.

It was the death of Thomas Jefferson's daughter Maria that reconciled the Adamses to the opposition president. Informed of her death, Mrs. Adams wrote a note of condolence, reminding their former friend how the then little girl had lived with the Adamses in London for awhile and on parting had wept: "Oh! now I have learned to love you, why will they take me from you?"[19] Political paranoia on either side could not withstand that.

That did not mean abandoning politics. She devoted those energies to shaping the career of John Quincy to become our sixth President. She urged his wife to make sure he did not work himself to death in the Senate, that he had a proper diet, that he took care of his personal appearance. "I wish you would not let him go to congress without a cracker in his pocket."[20]

Death of son Charles from dissipation at age 30 meant looking after his widow and family, too. By 1800, however, Abigail Adams welcomed them with grandmotherly affection. With 16 of her own grandchildren she would become expert. She speaks of her neighbor as being "encumbered with children," then catches herself: "Why should I say encumbered; doth not the Scripture say that children are an Heritage of the Lord?"[21] And she meant it.

She delighted in corresponding with the children, especially little Caroline, Nabby's daughter, whose chit-chat letters "amuse and divert us, so lively so gay, like the bird which hops from spray to spray and carols as he sits imparting pleasure to his fellow songsters."[22] About the grandchildren altogether she said, "I would feel quite melancholy without them."[23]

"You would wonder how I can write a line," she would say, "surrounded and interrupted 20 times within this hour — Here comes little John: 'Grandmamma, I have lost my [pennies] in the grass....Now I can't buy me a sword. Won't you give me another?"[24]

"'Hush, child, don't you see I am writing?'

"Then in runs Elizabeth holding up her little arms for me to take her. 'Away with you all! or I will lock the door.'" No wonder she apologizes, "This letter has lain unfinished for several days—"

And little William, Caroline's brother. Grandmamma Adams reports: "William came from his [other] grandmamma's [house] an almost ruined child, but I have brought him to be a fine boy now."[25]

With passage of time, Nabby died of breast cancer (in 1813 at age 38) and Caroline assumed the role of advisee, clearly with a girl's impatience of preaching. Grandmamma must remind her that this is what grandmothers are supposed to do: "I treasure up and venerate many of the maxims of my good grandmother Quincy as the most precious of relics" because she, too, remembered that she was once young.[26]

On the Adamses' fiftieth wedding anniversary, she confessed to Caroline, "The greatest source of unhappiness" during their marriage rose "from the long and cruel separations which I was called in a time of war, and with a young family around me, to submit to."[27] And when Caroline became a bride herself, John Adams tendered this grandfatherly advice about the children to come:

"Be sure to make them all, male and female, children, grandchildren, and great grandchildren, work hard with their own hands so as to be able to command their own livelihood by their industry, economy, and sagacity."[28] That would be replaying his wife's own life.

She had died of a lingering fever in late October 1818 knowing intuitively that John Adams would outlive her, yet satisfied with the life they had built together. Her aim at the end as at the beginning and in between remained consistent — to be his helpmate. Her highest ambition, she had told him, was to be just that. "A well ordered home is my chief delight and the affectionate domestic wife with the relative duties which accompany that character my highest ambition."[29]

Visitors to Braintree in her later years were thus charmed

to find that the elderly ex-President always appeared "an equal and friend who had lived himself into one with the wife of his bosom."[30] They would find her "in the dress of the matrons" of an earlier New England, "the black bonnet, the short cloak, the gown open before, and quilted petticoat, and the high-heeled shoe." There was Abigail Adams shelling beans for the family dinner.

Excerpts from Abigail Adams' Letters

[My selection focuses first on her residence in France and England in the mid-Eighties and then on her letters to granddaughter Caroline Smith who published them herself in 1841. The letters from grandson Charles Francis Adams' edition of 1840 were addressed to her two sisters or their daughters.]

1784, Auteuil, four miles from Paris

[September 5 to sister Mary Cranch about setting up housekeeping abroad:] I have a French girl about nineteen, whom I have been upon the point of turning away, because Madame will not brush a chamber; "it is not de fashion, it is not her business." I would not have kept her a day longer, but found, upon inquiry, that I could not do better myself, and hair-dressing here is very expensive, unless you keep such a madam in the house. She sews tolerably well, so I make her useful as I can. She is more particularly devoted to Mademoiselle [young Abby, 19]. Esther [her maid] diverted me yesterday evening by telling me that she heard her go muttering by her chamber door after she had been assisting Abby in dressing. "Ah, mon Dieu, 'tis provoking" — she talks a little English. "Why, what is the matter, Pauline, what is provoking?" "Why, Mademoiselle look so pretty, I so mauvais.". . .

I have become steward and book-keeper, determined to know with accuracy what our expenses are and to prevail with Mr. Adams to return to America if he finds himself straitened, as I think he must be. Mr. Jay went home because he could not support his family here with the whole salary; what then can be done, curtailed as it now is, with the additional expense? Mr. Adams is determined to keep as little company as he possibly can, but some entertainments we must make, and it is no unusual thing for them to amount to fifty or sixty guineas at a time. More is to be performed by way of negotiation, many times, at one of these entertainments than at twenty serious conversations; but the policy of our country has been and still is to be penny-wise and pound-foolish.

We stand in sufficient need of economy, and, in the curtailment of other salaries, I suppose they thought it absolutely necessary to cut off their foreign ministers. But, my own interest apart, the system is bad; for that nation which degrades their own ministers by obliging them to live in narrow circumstances, cannot expect to be held in high estimation themselves. We spend no evenings abroad, make no suppers, attend very few public entertainments, or spectacles, as they are called, and avoid every expense that is not held indispensable. Yet I cannot but think it hard that a gentleman who has devoted so great a part of his life to the service of the public, who has been the means in great measure of procuring such extensive territories to his country, who saved their fisheries, and who is still laboring to procure the further advantages should find it necessary so cautiously to calculate his pence, for fear of overrunning them. . . .

I long to hear from you. House and garden, with all its decoration, are not so dear to me as my own little cottage, connected with the society I used there to enjoy; for, out of my own family, I have no attachments in Europe, nor do I think I ever shall have. As to the language, I speak it a little bad grammar and all; but I have so many French servants that I am under a necessity of trying. . . . [191-97]

[Writing the same day to niece Lucy Cranch:] As to the people here, they are more given to hospitality than in England, it is said. I have been in company with but one French lady since I arrived; for strangers here make the first visit, and nobody will know you until you have waited upon them in form.

This lady [Madame Helvétius] I dined with at Dr. Franklin's. She entered the room with a careless, jaunty air; upon seeing ladies who were strangers to her, she bawled out, "Ah! mon Dieu, where is Franklin? Why did you not tell me there were ladies here?" You must suppose her speaking all this in French. "How I look!" said she, taking hold of a chemise made of tiffany, which she had on over a blue lutestring, and which looked as much upon the decay as her beauty, for she was once a handsome woman; her hair was frizzled; over it she had a small straw hat, with a dirty gauze half-handkerchief round it, and a bit of dirtier gauze than ever my maids wore, was bowed on behind. She had a black gauze scarf thrown over her shoulders.

She ran out of the room. When she returned, the Doctor entered at one door, she at the other; upon which she ran forward to him, caught him by the hand, "Hélas! Franklin – " then gave him a double kiss, one upon each cheek and another upon his forehead. When we went into the room to dine, she was placed between the Doctor and Mr. Adams. She carried on the chief of the conversation at dinner, frequently locking her hand into the Doctor's and sometimes spreading her arms upon the backs of both the gentlemen's chairs, then throwing her arm carelessly upon the Doctor's neck.

I should have been greatly ashamed at this conduct, if the good Doctor had not told me that in this lady I should see a genuine Frenchwoman, wholly free from affectation or stiffness of behaviour, and one of the best women in the world. For this I must take the Doctor's word; but I should have set her down for a very bad one, although sixty years of age, and a widow. I own I was highly disgusted and never wish for an acquaintance with any ladies of this cast.

After dinner she threw herself upon a settee, where she showed more than her feet. She had a little lap-dog who was, next to the Doctor, her favorite. This she kissed, and when he wet the floor, she wiped it up with her chemise. This is one of the Doctor's most intimate friends, with whom he dines once a week, and she with him. She is rich and is my near neighbour; but I have not yet visited her. Thus you see, my dear, that manners differ exceedingly in different countries. I hope, however, to find amongst the French ladies manners more consistent with my ideas of decency or I shall be a mere recluse. . . .[198-200]

[Still on the same day, 5 September, she writes to her learned friend Mercy Otis Warren about the contrast between Britain and France, wishing she could join the cleanliness of the one with the civility and politeness of the other, then adding a note about politics:] As to politics, madam, the world is at peace, and I have wholly done with them. Your good husband and mine would speculate upon treaties of commerce could they spend their evenings together, as I sincerely wish they could, or upon what they love better, agriculture and husbandry, which is become full as necessary for our country.

This same surly John Bull is kicking up the dust and growling, looking upon the fat pastures he has lost, with a malicious and envious eye; and though he is offered admission upon decent terms, he is so mortified and stomachful that, although he longs for a morsel, he has not yet agreed for a single bite. . . .[203]

[The letter remained unsent, so she added more on 12 December:] Since it was written there have been some changes in the political world, and the emperor [of Germany] has recalled his ambassador from the United Provinces. Everything seems to wear a hostile appearance. The Dutch are not in the least intimidated but are determined at all events to refuse the opening of the Scheldt to the emperor. This court is endeavoring to mediate between the emperor and the Dutch. When the affair was to be debated in the king's council, the queen said to this Count de Vergennes, "M. le Comte, you must remember that the emperor is my brother." "I certainly shall, Madam," replied the Count; "but your majesty will remember that you are the queen of France." Thus much for Politics. [205- 6]

1785 Auteuil

[On the eve of leaving Auteuil, she writes to Mrs. Cranch:] Can my dear sister realize that it is near eleven months since I left her? To me it seems incredible; more like a dream than reality. Yet it ought to appear the longest ten months of my life if I were to measure the time by the variety of objects which have occupied my attention; but, amidst them all, my heart returns, like the dove of Noah, and rests only in my native land. I never thought myself so selfish a being as since I have become a traveller; for, although I see nature around me in a much higher state of cultivation than our own country can boast, and elegance of taste and manners in a thousand forms, I cannot feel interested in them. . . .

I have bought a little bird lately, and I really think I feel more attached to that than to any object out of my own family, animate or inanimate. Yet I do not consider myself in the predicament of a poor fellow who, not having a house in which to put his head, took up his abode in the stable of a gentleman; but, though so very poor, he kept a dog with whom he daily divided the small portion of food which he earned. Upon being asked why, when he found it so difficult to live himself, he still kept a dog. "What," says the poor fellow, "part with my dog! Why, whom should I have to love me then?". . . .[247-48]

1785 London

[A few weeks after John Adams was received as America's ambassador to the Court of St. James, Mrs. Adams and daughter Abby were presented to the King and Queen, as she reports to sister Mary in late June:] We were placed in a circle round the drawing-room, which was very full, I believe two hundred persons present. Only think of the task! The royal family have to go round to every person and find small talk enough to speak to all of them, though they very prudently speak in a whisper, so that only the person who stands next you can hear what is said. The King enters the room and goes round to the right; the Queen and the Princesses to the left. . . .

When [George the Third] came to me, Lord Onslow said, "Mrs. Adams," upon which I drew off my right-hand glove and his Majesty saluted [kissed] my left cheek, then asked me if I had taken a walk today. I could have told his Majesty that I had been all the morning preparing to wait upon him, but I replied, "No, Sire." "Why, don't you love walking?" says he. I answered that I was rather indolent in that respect. He then bowed and passed on.

It was more than two hours after this before it became my turn to be presented to the Queen. The circle was so large that the company were four hours standing. The Queen was evidently embarrassed when I was presented to her. I had disagreeable feelings too. She, however, said "Mrs. Adams, have you got into your house? Pray, how do you like the situation of it?" Whilst the Princess Royal looked compassionate and asked me if I was not much fatigued, and observed that it was a very full drawing-room. Her sister, who came next, Princess Augusta, after having asked [young Abby] if she was ever in England before, and her answering "Yes," inquired of me how long ago, and supposed it was when she was very young. And all this said with much affability and the ease and freedom of old acquaintance. . . .

As to the ladies of the Court, rank and title may compensate for want of personal charm, but they are, in general, very plain, ill shaped, and ugly; but don't tell anybody that I say so. . . . The Tories are very free with their compliments. Scarcely a paper escapes without some scurrility. We bear it with silent contempt, having met a polite reception from the Court, it bites them like a serpent and stings them like an adder. . . .[256-58]

1809 Quincy, Massachusetts — Letters to Caroline

[Mrs. Adams' Abby had wed William Smith in 1786 and birthed a succession of boys until February 1795 when baby Caroline arrived, to become the favorite grandchild of Mrs. Adams. Caroline, her brothers, and cousins Susan and Abby, children of the late Charles Adams, and sometimes John Quincy Adams' children John and George all lived with their grandmother during the time the following letters were written. Fittingly, it was Caroline who brought Mrs. Adams her first great-grandchild in September 1816 and then went on to edit her grandmother's letters as Caroline de Windt in 1841 — as excerpted here:]

December 9. Thursday, 30th November, was our Thanksgiving Day; I was not able to attend church, owing to my eye, which I regretted: our good minister is always excellent upon particular occasions; I am told he was upon this.

At dinner I looked round, I hope with a thankful heart, but alas! how many of my dear children were absent, not one of them to give pleasure to the festive table; the young shoots and branches remained; I had two from each family; these promising successors of their dear parents rejoiced over their plum-puddings without knowing what were the reflections and anxious solicitude of their grandmother, respecting some of their absent parents.

For health, food, and raiment, for peace, and for society, and unnumbered other favours, may my heart pour forth its grateful effusions. . . . No apology is ever necessary to my dear Caroline for any serious reflections which may fall from the pen of her aged grandmother; reflection becomes all ages, and she does not the less delight in the innocent gayety and vivacity of youth. . . .

I am rejoiced to find that you intend to turn your spinning wheel; the more we are qualified to help ourselves, the less dependent we are upon others; from the present temper of old England, it looks as if we should be less her customers than formerly. I would recommend the use of them in every family. We had better return to the pastoral age than suffer the domination of any foreign power.

It is said that the Emperor Augustus wore no clothes but such as were made by the Empress and her daughters; and Olympias did the same for Alexander. The web of Penelope is well known to you, as related by Homer in his Odyssey; her maids who attended her are admonished by Ulysses to retire with her . . . "Go with the Queen, the spindle guide or cull, (The partners of her cares) the silver wool."

Thus, my dear girl, you have before you some of the most ancient, illustrious examples to excite your ambition and imitation. Your mother accuses me of neglect in her education upon this head, and I plead guilty to the charge; I would, by my advice to you, endeavour to rectify my deficiency towards her. . . . [219- 20]

1814 Quincy

[In mid-September ugly duckling Caroline wed a wealthy Columbia classmate of her brother's and went to reside at his estate in Fishkill, New York, where she lived happily ever after. Her grandmother wrote on September 27th, a week after the wedding:] We were all delighted; grandfather's tears watered his cheek when he read the letter [about her new home]; Susan skipped with all her warmth and ardour into every part of the scene... walked her mile and a half to communicate the grateful tidings; every heart and eye participated with you.

I shall not say anything about the wonders of the world, for this reason, I know not what to say; yet I cannot help feeling pity or commisseration for Buonaparte; to what part of the world can he flee? Some say America! I do not want him here, although I think he would be quite harmless, deprived as he is of all power, authority and means.

By the help of one night's refreshing sleep, I am enabled to write to you this morning, knowing not what the morrow may bring forth. Four score and ten is an age when we can neither expect health or much strength, when our strength is weakness. I cannot say that I have no pleasure in my days; I have abundant in this, my sickness. I have had kind, attentive friends, a skilful physician, and every human aid: is there not pleasure in all this? and unto the Great First Cause be the praise.

Dear, tempting child, how pleased I should be to make you the visit you so pathetically [feelingly] urge; but would it not be too hazardous for your grandfather, at his age, to undertake? True, we enjoy much health, and as good spirits as can be expected, and more than we had reason to look for, considering the many scenes we have passed through; but we must finish our course in our own habitation and not venture beyond a day's journey. I might be hazardous enough to run the risk, but I would not have your grandfather, who may yet outlive me, though so many years older. [225-27]

[The next month, October 23, she talks about the death of her old friend Mercy Warren:] I may with truth say that, take her all in all, we shall not look upon her like again. String after string is severed from the heart; the lamp of life burnt bright to the last. Dr. Freeman told me she wrote him a letter upon the 6th of the present month, when she entered her 87th year. I rejoice that you visited her; your remembrance of her will always be pleasant. Seldom does old age wear so pleasing, so instructive an aspect. To me she was a friend of more than fifty summers ripening.

Yesterday completed half a century since I entered the married state, then just your age. I have great cause of thankfulness that I have lived so long and enjoyed so large a portion of happiness as has been my lot. The greatest source of unhappiness I have known in that period was arisen from the long and cruel separations which I was called in a time of war, and with a young family around me, to submit to.

My pen runs on, "but," as the gallant Adam said to Eve, "with thee conversing I forget all time."

That you and the rest of my posterity may enjoy as large a share of felicity as has fallen to me is the sincere wish and prayer of your affectionate grandmother, A.A. [229-30]

Mary Morris, from an engraving of the painting
by C.W. Peale

MARY WHITE MORRIS

Born Philadelphia, 13 April 1749.

Died Philadelphia, 16 January 1827, active to the end.

Younger of two children born to Colonel Thomas White, surveyor- general of Baltimore County, and his second wife, Esther Huelings Newman White.

Wed Robert Morris, 2 March 1769.

Seven children — Robert, Junior (1769-1804), Thomas (1771-1849), William (1772-1798), Hetty (1774-1795), Charles (1777-c.1800), Maria (1779-1852), Henry (1784-1842).

Supported husband for remainder of his life after debtors prison.

MARY WHITE MORRIS

May 1789, on the way to join the new president in New York, Martha Washington stopped over in Philadelphia to pick up her dear friend Molly Morris. The two shared a passion for staying at home and both willingly sacrificed their private lives to satisfy their husbands' commitment to service. Mrs. Robert Morris thus accompanied Mrs. George Washington to New York and for the duration of Washington's presidency would sit at her right hand at various social functions. Molly Morris served as ghost hostess for her less sophisticated friend.

At home she had to play busy hostess for her ambitious, gregarious husband while trying to raise seven children, most of them two years apart. As wealthiest Philadelphians when the city was second-largest in the British empire, the Morrises hosted foreign visitors of any importance — although as often as not he was away from home on business, putting the burden of entertaining on his wife.

She had been brought up to that kind of role. She had the model of her mother, Esther Hewlings Newman White, who had performed the same service for the last twenty years of his life for a husband crippled from a fall, yet almost as gregarious as son-in-law Morris.[1] Molly's brother Billy would grow up to become the nation's presiding Episcopal bishop, attributing his common-sense, unostentatious piety to his mother.[2] Her own family, early converts from Quakerism, retained some of the objections to such nonsense as playgoing, gambling, or dancing, but Mrs. White had enough confidence in her children's good nature to give them free rein.

Inheriting her mother's quiet grace and tall, elegant bearing, Molly moved easily in Philadelphia society of the 60s. A measure of her popularity among the young people is the fact that her name led the list of Philadelphia belles in society verse of the period:

> In lovely White's most pleasing form,
> What various graces meet,
> How blest with every striking charm,
> How languishingly sweet.[3]

Her brunette beauty with an innate dignity and grace attracted ambitious, physically imposing Robert Morris who, at 35, having acquired a small fortune in overseas trading, now felt the need to found a dynasty of his own. She was 19 when they wed.

Robert Morris had risen quickly from apprentice in the leading merchant firm of the Willing family to form a partnership with Thomas Willing. Willing provided the venture capital, Morris the talent. He would sail with their ships overseas, cementing the personal contacts so solidly that soon his word alone could seal a deal. That is why he was able to almost single-handedly rescue the Revolution from financial failure, pledging $1,400,000 of his own bonds — all of which he would redeem.[4] Later, as superintendent of finance, he would reduce the cost of government from $18,000,000 to $5,000,000 in just three years (1781-84).

Goals of this sort required the kind of effort that turns a person into a workaholic. He was offered the presidency of Congress but turned it down to take care of his own business, a mixed blessing to Molly Morris. She joked to her mother: "Don't you feel quite important? I assure you I do, and begin to be reconciled to Independence."[5] He would be away from home just as much.

Besides the long periods of separation caused by the War, the fever seasons would drive her and the children into retreats with Mrs. White in Maryland or their own home near Lancaster or their summer place in what is now Philadelphia's Fairmount Park. This meant Molly Morris becoming the equivalent of a workaholic as a letter writer, partly to keep Morris in touch with their brood and also to keep him informed of local politics. This is the same kind of information she would send to her mother, other members of the family, and intimate friends like Sally Livingston Jay, whose sister Kitty lived with the Morrises while the Jays were in Europe.

To her mother in Maryland she delighted in sending news of national importance that also touched the family — as when brother Billy was to be named chaplain to Congress. News of society and fashion took second place to politics. Molly Morris reported the engagement of Benedict Arnold along with descriptions of military balls just after the British evacuated Philadelphia: "Our military gentlemen here are too liberal," she said, for they make no distinction between those girls who fraternized with the enemy and those who remained loyal Whigs. In fact, she added, they seemed to favor the Tories — "strange as it may seem" that is the way of the world in Philadelphia.[6]

She and Sally Jay kept up an exchange of such comments leavened with fun and the obligatory reports on fashions on both sides of the Atlantic, along with plenty of serious discussion. When Morris agreed to be superintendent of finance, Sally was quick to urge his wife to make sure he took time off: "Your fears for Mr. Morris' health are, I own, too well founded."[7] She knew that from experience with a workaholic husband of her own, and so she urged taking him "into the country, at least of evenings," persuading him it was the patriotic thing to do.

Molly kept silent about her routine patriotic duties. By nature a pacifist who could not celebrate American victories when loss of life occurred, she nevertheless went door-to-door with other members of the local Ladies association shyly collecting money for the boys at the front — "some carrying inkstands, nor did they let the meanest ale house escape."[8]

Nor did she bore Mrs. Jay with the lively social life she had to lead as Mrs. Superintendent of Finance, spouse of the town's wealthiest financier and thus the one person every visiting celebrity had to see first. Some of that priority rubbed off, as when the new French ambassador insisted on escorting her at his first reception, or visiting French royalty tangled with unexpected Yankee elegance.[9]

The Prince de Broglie, delighted with the shiny mahogany furnishings and brilliantly polished brass of the Morris home, suffered a little culture shock at tea: "I should be even now drinking it, I believe, if the Ambassador had not charitably notified me at the twelfth cup that I must put my spoon across it when I wished to finish." Molly Morris' reports were more dramatic than that, as in telling Sally Jay about the duel between two Frenchmen:

They took their places and each took turns firing. "One fired and missed. The other placed his pistol on his antagonist's forehead who had just enough time to say, 'Ah, mon Dieu, pardonnez-moi!' at the same time bowing. The pistol went off and did no other damage than singeing a few of his hairs."[10]

Their letters took on more poignancy after November 1781 when two of her sons were sent to the Continent for their education that had been interrupted by the war. Ten-year-old Thomas and eleven-year-old Robert would spend the next half-dozen years abroad, causing Molly Morris untold anxiety, since she tried hard to suppress it from them.

At vacations, the boys would visit Paris and Sally Jay could keep her informed of their growing maturity. When they were headed back to school, John Jay tried to extract a promise they would write at least once every fortnight. Robert readily agreed, but Thomas hesitated, reported Mrs. Jay, because writing once a fortnight was too tough a task.[11]

This kind of report moved Mrs. Morris to share a fantasy. "How," she asked Mrs. Jay, "would you like to change situations with me for a few days on a visit to those you love here, and I be transported to Paris on the same charming errand, occupying each others bodies to prevent any derangement that might happen in our families in consequence of our absence but preserving our own sensibilities?"[12]

Then reality set in: "Before I had penned my thought, two objections started — the first that I should not see you, the second that I might become so enamoured with my new form as to be discontented with my own."

To the boys themselves she wrote constantly. Their father would send words of encouragement and sententious advice, leaving to her news of family and friends. Wishing Robert a happy seventeenth birthday: "When seated with our little family round the breakfast table this morning, I announced to them that this was their brother Robert's birthday. They asked so many questions as to prolong their meal so long, I was obliged to remind them that it was time to go to school."[13]

Then, as if to emphasize the length of separation without complaining about it, she added that baby Henry, who was two-and-a-half and thus had been born after they'd left Philadelphia, "believes that he knows his absent brothers, and although he speaks only a few words, yet he . . . imagines that he is well acquainted with you." Robert and Thomas were away at school for seven years, 1781-88.

Typically, when they finally reached home, their father was down South taking care of business with his close friend (but no kin) Gouverneur Morris, speculating in undeveloped land. Separation for war or public service was one thing, but extended business trips for speculating by a man who had more wealth than most other men exasperated Molly Morris, then made her miserable. Previously she had begun her letters to him, "Dear Mr. Morris." Now it was "My Dearest Friend." "I do not love writing," she told him, but now writing had become "my most pleasing employment, it being the only way I have of conversing with you."[14]

First she tried what sarcasm would do, talking about seeing a man who had seen him more recently than she had heard from him: "I must say that I never found Mr. Pollock so agreeable before as in a long Conversation I have had with him . . . . He told me much more about you than I have heard from any other Person since you left."

Sarcasm was not her nature, however, and she went on: "I am again disappointed my beloved friend in not receiving by last night's mail a letter from you . . . . It is indeed too long now that you have been absent from us. I find my patience, my dear Mr. Morris, most exhausted . . . O my dearest partner, how my heart yearns for your return to enjoy with me the society of our amiable family."

To see that this was not the typical lamenting letter of the times, contrast it with one by her sister-in-law Mary White to William White while he was in England seeking ordination: "I should go on scribling every day, whether you think it worth reading or not."[15]

Mary White goes on to explain that writing is therapy: "God only knows the pangs this separation had caused me, as well as how great my struggles have been to keep myself from sinking under it. When I think of my children, and what their situation might be should I suffer myself to be depress'd to that degree that I could not act for them as I now find I must in a double capacity, it rouses me when everything else fails."

By contrast, Molly Morris could be funny with her errant spouse. She apologized for not at once answering his "tender and affectionate" letter in kind because she has "a provoking head-ach" but then goes on at great length to talk politics:

"As you know that I am something of a Politician I therefore could not forebear informing you that the Federal Government is agreed to by our convention." The real point of the letter is to tell him that the jubilant crowd "did not forget YOU" — they marched to the Morris house to give three cheers, and she probably gave them good cheer in return.[16]

In financial recessions of 1796-97, Morris's losses were catastrophic. He had bought up more land in what would become the District of Columbia than all other purchasers combined, yet could sell hardly any while interest on his high-risk loans accumulated and his fortune decayed. His mammoth speculation went on so high a scale that all Europe trembled at his fall. He had sold 1,200,000 acres of Massachusetts land alone in Europe.[17] Failure of his London banker coupled with fraud on the part of his New York City partner James Greenleaf finally ruined him.

When Morris went to debtors prison, the family lost friends as well as fortune. One friend said, "Adversity has soured them and they view men and things through a partial medium and weigh everything by their own sufferings."[18] But Morris's letters sent from prison reveal just the opposite. His chief concern after his family's welfare was to ease the losses of his smaller investors, and to this end he kept Robert busy trying to negotiate their relief. Thomas, now a New York state legislator, later a congressman, did what he could to salvage the New York properties. Molly looked after the rest of the family.

At the height of their prosperity a joke in Philadelphia maintained that Hetty and Maria would never marry since it would mean their husbands would have to marry the whole family. Hetty did make a very successful marriage with James Marshall, younger brother of the celebrated jurist John Marshall, and now lived in Winchester, Virginia. With Mrs. White dead, it was Hetty who offered retreat from the fever season. From Winchester it was easy riding to Mount Vernon and reunion with Martha Washington and her husband — who on an official visit to Philadelphia took time to see Robert Morris in debtors prison.[19]

During Morris's three-and-a-half years in prison his wife

remained his chief concern: "Separation from her is the hardest thing to bear."[20] Thanks to old friend Gouverneur Morris, she negotiated an annuity from the Holland Land Company. Under his tutelage she simply refused to sign some necessary papers until they concurred with the terms she proposed. In this way she secured an income enabling her to take a small house near the prison to await his release.

Every day she and daughter Maria would visit Robert Morris in his prison room which they reached only through a long, hot, humid corridor. In Philadelphia summers marked by malignant fevers, this meant threading their way through festering corpses that lined each side of the corridor, piled floor to ceiling.

Morris would send letters of advice to the children even from jail. When Maria visited her sister in Virginia, she received a four-page, closely packed letter on the need for females to educate themselves through wide and deep reading. It concluded, however, by warning that "an affected, learned lady that reads only to make display is detested."[21]

Twenty-year-old Maria could take care of herself. Two of her brothers caused her mother great grief. During the first months of Morris's imprisonment, 26-year-old William succumbed to fever.[22] Not long after that, fourth son Charles who had joined the Navy, lived a dissolute life, and deserted, finally dropped out of sight forever.[23]

Released under a new bankruptcy law in 1801, Robert Morris could not find work.[24] Molly Morris supported him for the rest of his life on her small annuity. Except for occasional visits to old friends like Gouverneur Morris, he would stay indoors plotting new plans until at 70, weakened by years in prison, he died. Left unfinished were plans for a retirement community in North Florida.[25]

His death in 1806 did nothing to decrease the flow of legal claims against his estate, such as it was. But by now Molly Morris had two lawyers in the family — sons-in-law James Marshall and Henry Nixon — besides politicians Gouverneur Morris and her sons Thomas and Robert, both in Washington. She could thus retire into the life she had always wished for, calm, serene, comfortable. She kept so low a profile that the world would not have known she was still around if Lafayette had not stopped off in Philadelphia on his triumphant return to this country.

In September 1824 he arrived to wild acclaim at five in the afternoon, made obligatory remarks to the crowd, then immediately asked to be taken to the home of his old friend's widow, Mrs. Robert Morris.[26] Once again singled out as first among Philadelphiennes, she responded as of old by doing her duty to society, attending the grand ball given in his honor, her last appearance in public.

She died at 78 in January 1827. Her obituary reported that her greatest pleasure since Morris's death had been hearing from young people whose lives he had changed for the better.[27] The same could be said of her, his dearest friend.

Extracts from Mary Morris' Letters

> The first extracts showing her reacting to wartime, and the others, relating to her sons' absence abroad and their return, are all normalized from the Huntington Library manuscripts.

1777 Bushtown, Maryland

[A refugee from fighting in Philadelphia, she writes to her husband from sanctuary in rural Maryland, 28 February:] Anxious you should know what I determine on about coming up [to Philadelphia], I set down immediately to write a few lines for that purpose . . . It's probable it may meet with one of the Congress as they are now moving up [from Annapolis] to Philadelphia. The roads, Mr. Purviance says, are impassable for carriages and baggage, so had you determined on your first pleasing plan, my dear, it could not have been executed at present. But I shall comply with your last determination of coming myself with this difference — of leaving our darling daughter and bringing [baby] Tom on account of his sore, which is not yet healed and requires the attendance of his mother and the skill of a physician, which he can be better supplied with there than here.

What a variety of sensations, my dearest husband, have your different determinations excited in me this day. Your first, wrote of the twenty-first, was so unexpected but yet so pleasing — to be summoned home — to the enjoyment of your company. Immediately, in the next sheet, damped by your disappointment in the waggoner and by the most objectionable of all disappointments, danger of the enemy. And the last of all, one just brought me . . . desiring me to postpone moving till I hear further from you, which has altered my intentions from what they were as I sat down to tell you that I should soon have the inexpressible joy of meeting you in Philadelphia. [HM 9923]

1781 Springetsbury, suburban Philadelphia

[After responding to Sally Jay's thanks for looking after her sister Kitty, Mrs. Morris comments on three shiploads of refugees, 29 July 1781:] Three flags [ships] have just arrived from Charleston, South Carolina, sent by the British for the purposes of conveying hither the first families of that place, that they may get rid of persons who they have so inhumanely plundered of their estates and thereby be excused from allowing the small pittance they proposed for their subsistence.

There is no instance of greater tyranny than has been exercised to these people, very unlike a generous foe who would admire the laudable pride that kept them from asking favors or associating with the enemies of their country. The effects were very different on those domineering Britons, for they very soon declared their intention of subduing the haughty spirit of the Carolinians, for that they asked favors more like the conquerors than the conquered.

They put them on board small vessels, and so crowded that had their bad fortune still pursued them in a long passage, infectious disorders were very much to be apprehended in the month of July, and their poor emaciated bodies must soon have submitted to such a foe. I was very much surprised to find them in such good spirits. Observing it, they declared they experienced a degree of happiness beyond what they thought their situation admitted of, that breathing free air, meeting with a hospitable reception from their countrymen, and coming to a land of plenty had given them joyous hearts, though they had not a farthing to purchase the fine beef and mutton which they eagerly hastened to market to see soon after their arrival.

However, I hope that humanity and generosity will continue to show themselves a characteristic of this country, and cheerfully execute the plan of Congress for a loan to relieve their necessities as the most delicate way of doing it, and the one they prefer. — The situation of these poor people occupy my thoughts so much that I find my time I allowed for writing is elapsed without saying many things I intended. . . . [HM 13507]

1783 Philadelphia

June 1. [To Mrs. Jay:] I congratulate you on peace being

restored to our country; it was hardly announced to us before the flags [ships] of different nations crowded into our Port and made us immediately sensible of its great advantages, for the importance of the subject so bewildered us at first like a charming revery that we wished to indulge and were afraid, but no sooner roused than we felt every moment more sensible the happy change.

In the course of this winter I have written to my dear Mrs. Jay two or three times and am afraid those letters met with the common fate of being taken. If that is the case, unless you know my heart, you must be ignorant of the grateful sense I have of yours and Mr. Jay's attention to my dear boys. Indeed I cannot suppose but that you know me better, without giving myself credit for more penetration in character than you know, as from my knowledge of you I was sure on your arriving in Paris my children would meet in you the best of friends.

Dear little fellows, I should be glad to know from your candid pen if they are pleased with their situation. For, if it be otherwise they are too good to write to us so.... [HM 13519]

[For Mrs. Jay's reports on the boys, see the extracts from her letters for 1782 and 1783 below.]

1786 Philadelphia

December 19. [To her eldest son, Robert Junior, at the University of Leipzig:] This day my dear Robert is the anniversary of that which gave you birth. . . . I hope I flatter myself that your next will be spent in the bosom of your family. Five of them have now elapsed since our separation. When seated with our little family round the breakfast table this morning, I announced to them that this was their brother Robert's birthday. It was startling for their little imaginations; so pleasing a subject for the enquiries of a brother that they love as to prolong their meal so long as obliged me to remind them that it was time to go to school. Even little Henry, by his little affections, took a part, for he believes that he knows his absent brothers, and though he speaks only a very few words, yet from being so taught, imagines that he is well acquainted with you. [HM 13530]

1787

[Succeeding extracts are from letters to her husband, all from Philadelphia while he remains away from home on business. This one is a newsy note dating from 11 December:] I had not room to add in the enclosed sheet that the war which it is believed has commenced between France and England is the universal topic of conversation here. Doctor Franklin is of opinion that America from the present power of Great Britain has also much to fear. *He* regrets very much having laid one brick upon another as we are so entirely in a defenceless state. [HM 13524]

December 12. As you know . . . I am something of a politician and could not forbear informing you that the federal government is agreed to by our [Constitutional state ratifying] convention. They finished last evening. Great demonstrations of joy were expressed by the populace. They did not forget YOU. We had three cheers. . . .

My equally dear friend and partner, your hiring a house and laying in provision for your horses [in Richmond, Virginia] damps my expectations. . . . Nothing but its being so necessary to your quiet can reconcile me to so long an absence. The children are all well and at school except your little Captain [i.e., three-year-old Henry] who, dear little fellow, I am obliged to banish from the room while I write. [HM 13533]

1788

January 13. The arrival of the English packet [i.e., the ship from England] has been for some time expected. I am very desirous for it to arrive, expecting to hear from our boys. I sincerely, hope that you are mistaken in believing them to be not in England. I wish very much it may be so. I should like them for to see that country. I think too they might employ their time to more purpose than it appears they were likely to do in Leipsig. We shall see them, you think, in May. It is indeed a very desirable meeting after an absence of six years with such amiable children as we have every reason to believe them to be. If I hear from them in England, I shall be then more certain of the time of their return and shall almost count the moments till they restore to my embraces, those dear objects of my attention.

But believe me, there is an absent one whose return is still more necessary to my happiness than even that of my dear children. But the time is not so far off now before I shall have you again — sometime in the month of February, I hope, at farthest, hoping by that time you will have got through your business, for as much as I long for your return, I am clearly of opinion for you not to leave an account unsettled that should require your presence, or to harass your mind. . . .

I now know from experience how in future to be very careful in giving those French friends of our an invitation to lodge. When I made the offer to Monsieur Le Couteulx [former Paris banker] for his lady, it was only meant for the night after the concert that she said she was so desirous to come to. That being the case, think of my surprise at being told by Mr. [William Temple] Franklin that she proposed spending with me several days, and it's my opinion that if I had proposed her remaining here and not going home at all till after the ball, it would have been readily accepted. I thought so at the time but did not think it necessary to make such a sacrifice to my convenience.

She speaks so little of English yet that I had for to request of Mrs. Allen or Mr. Franklin, of one of them at a time, to be with me, for to converse with her. She is to be with me to dinner tomorrow. Mr. Penn has sent a card for her to a concert they are to have tomorrow evening, and I do very sincerely hope that she may return home to Farmer Le Couteulx (as the Frenchmen call him) the day after the ball — which said ball, by the by, is to be of all things the finest — 190 persons are asked. The preparations for and the high expectations furnish employment and conversation to everyone. I shall be less fearful of going, as there is to be so great a crowd, expecting it will make their rooms more bearable as with a smaller company they are bitter cold, as I found to my cost in drinking tea there last Saturday — and took a cold that I have not yet recovered. . . .

My children on Monday last was at a ball given by the little

Miss Chew. I was there too, invited by Mrs. Chew to see them, and a vast pleasure it is to see so large a collection of lovely children dance as well as they did. In your last letter you hit off exactly poor William's character. I was entertained very much by it, and the moreso as at this party at Mrs. Chew's I had seen such striking outlines of the just portrait you have drawn of him.

I did not know till on this occasion of your separation from us that he placed as I find he does your attention and approbation of his conduct, as of all others what he is most ambitious of. When he receives your letters, an expression of pleasure and satisfaction lights up his countenance such as I never saw produced in it by any other occasion. In short, I am very happy to find that he loves and respects you as you merit that he should. . . .

'Tis true I do not love writing, and that it was ever a task to me excepting in one instance, besides the present — I mean when we were before separated — and then it became as now, my most pleasing employment, it being the only way I have of conversing with you. If I could perform better in letter writing than I do, I should still feel it more agreeable, even to you, who I know will make every friendly allowance.

Mme. Le Couteulx did not come on Friday as I have wrote you she would in the preceding part of *this* [she is now writing on Sunday morning]. Monsieur Le Couteulx was sick, which prevented her then as she wrote me, and that I should see her to dinner today. Hetty was delighted to receive your letter which she would have answered, she says, today, had she been provided with a good pen. . . .

This day two months since you left us — as I observed it this morning when at breakfast, and our little children all agreed that they thought it at least four months. (Madame Le Couteulx is arrived.) [HM 13528]

March 29. By today's post I expect to hear from you from Richmond, and that the use of your finger is again entirely restored to you — informed as I am by Mr. Pollock, who got to town on Wednesday, that you arrived there the day before his departure. From him too I have the satisfaction to be informed that you were in perfect good health and spirits. I must say that I never found Mr. Pollock so agreeable before as in a long conversation I have had with him on your subject. I shall leave it to your penetration to discover why — But certain it is he told me much more about you than I have heard from any other person since you left me. . . .

Expecting as I think I may now daily the arrival of our boys was a motive to my not postponing of that [dinner] party, wishing no such clogs at present. The idea last night of their being on the coast, blowing a hurricane as it did from the south, made me suffer what no wind before ever did. My mind presented to me such scenes of horror which continued till about twelve oclock when the wind fell and I go to sleep. . . .

Finding that your finger was still so far from being in a state for to use your hand so much without being painful and inflaming it, that of the two evils, I had much rather forego that of not receiving your letters at present than that at the expense of furnishing me that pleasure you should protract its recovery. I am now at Sunday morning, and as I intend for church must bid you adieu for the present. The most fervent petition of my heart is that it may not be very long now that I have to say so to you, my very best and dearest friend. [HM 13523]

May 4. I am again disappointed, my beloved husband, in not receiving by last night's mail a letter from you, and the more so as Mr. Cotteringer tells me that the post passed through Richmond on his way up from Portsmouth. There has been time now for you to acknowledge the news of the arrival of your sons, and the last evening I hoped for to have received that pleasure, and also to have your determination whether I and the boys are to meet you at Mount Vernon or whether your return home will be so soon as to make it unnecessary — the last of which alternative I prefer at this time — although I should with pleasure, if I received your summons to do so, set off very expeditiously for to meet you the sooner and present to you my sons. For it is indeed too long now that you have been absent from us. I find my patience indeed, my dear Mr. Morris, most exhausted.

The French Minister, the marchioness his sister, her son

the Count Breon, and the Minister's private secretary arrived in town the evening before last on a visit of five or six days. On the same evening we had a visit from the two young gentlemen. The next morning the boys waited on the Minister, and them and I on the marchioness, but did not see her. She was still in bed from the fatigue of her journey.

In the afternoon, she and the Minister, attended by a suite of Frenchmen, surprised me by an early visit and took tea with me. They had dined with the President [i.e., Benjamin Franklin, governor of Pennsylvania]. The marchioness is a very small woman exceedingly plain in her dress but of easy, agreeable manners and speaks tolerable English. The Count Moutier is a very comely man, plain in his dress and as little ceremony in his manners as a man can well have, or a Minister [of state]. Our sons are out with them now and have been since this morning at the request of the young gentlemen of their family to show them the country and the situations best worth seeing. The boys and myself are to dine today in company with them. . . .

I have not determined yet in what way, or on what day, for to give them an invitation, a trouble and expense I would gladly avoid. But if I cannot, shall see them with as little parade and expense as I possibly can. Had I last evening received your commands to depart for Virginia, as I had expectation of, I should have been out of the scrape.

I must, my dearest friend, bid you adieu . . . . The family are all of them well, and the home uncommonly quiet, none of the children but Henry being at home, and he in the yard under the willows, playing with Black Rachel. Hetty, Charles, and Maria are gone to church, and the three boys not yet returned from their escort. Nicholas procured Thomas a riding horse. Robert and William from sad necessity (preferring to ride) was obliged to take up with the phaeton and Nicholas to drive them.

O, my dearest partner, how my heart yearns for your return to enjoy with me the society of our amiable family of children. [HM 13542]

Sarah Jay

SARAH LIVINGSTON JAY

Born New York City, August 1757.

Died Bedford, New York, 28 May 1802, after "long, severe illness."

Fourth daughter of future Governor of New Jersey William Livingston and Susannah French Livingston; two brothers.

Wed John Jay, 28 April 1774.

Six children — Peter (1776-1843), Susan (1870-1780), Maria (1782-1856), Anna (1783-1856), William (1789-1858), Sarah Louisa (1792-1818).

Accompanied husband on foreign missions — 3 years in Spain, 1 year in France, one month in England (May 1782-June 1784).

SARAH LIVINGSTON JAY

During sensitive negotiations for peace with England, Franklin's house near Paris was daily made more exciting by John and Sally Jay's toddlers who stayed with the old man until their parents could get settled. Franklin and his Paris friends took great delight in watching so rare a sight as the amorous Americans, not because Jay's slender six-foot frame towered over diminutive Sally but because after ten years of marriage and three children they were still so manifestly in love.

One night while Jay had to stay in England, Franklin teased Sally with a pair of magnets. Before the assembled guests he placed one magnet near another, calling one John Jay and the other Sally. They were, she reported, "presently united," But then he replaced the Sally magnet with one representing "an English Lady" — "behold! the same effect. The Company," she said, "enjoyed it much and urged me to revenge, but all could not shake my confidence in my beloved friend."[1]

Despite surface appearances, this was no ingenue. Sally Jay was daughter of the wily politician New Jersey Governor William Livingston of the New York Livingstons. She inherited little of his extensive property — most of which he lost in the war — but she did inherit much of his wit and, alas, his explosive temper. The combination could be wicked. When she read in the newspapers that John Jay had been named president ofCongress without telling her, she fired off a missile:

"If you had consulted me, as some men have their wives about public [affairs], I should not have been Roman matron enough to have given you so entirely to the public."[2] Jay's reply reflects the reason their marriage remained so ideal. He pleaded guilty to neglect because he feared to think about her. The very thought of her "excited sensations very improper to be indulged in by a person in my station."

Taken seriously, however, her complaint foreshadowed the sporadic separations that marked the quarter-century of married bliss. She willingly followed him to Spain and France as she would have followed him to the ends of the earth. The places where their children were born reflects that fact: eldest son Peter — Elizabethtown, New Jersey at Governor Livingston's home while John Jay was with the Congress, 1776; Maria — Madrid, Spain six years later while Jay sought official recognition for the new nation; Anne — Passy, France, while he served on the peace commission, 1783; William and Sarah Louise — New York City, 1789 and 1792, while Jay served as Chief Justice of the United States Supreme Court.

They had married when he was 30 and she was only 18. She had already won a reputation as the local Kate as in Shakespeare's *Taming of the Shrew.* Family friend Gouverneur Morris vowed to one of her sisters, "I'll dispose of her before the Winter's out"[3] and he did, too, to his best friend John Jay, in 1774. Jay's kinder, gentler nature helped her to control her temper and to indulge her wit even at his expense. They could both laugh at her contradicting the "lord and master" as being "petty treason in the eye of every man who has the honor of being her husband."[4] She went on to play lovingly any role that would serve John Jay's career — business agent, gracious hostess, nonpolitical wife, and fulltime mother and father both.

With Jay away on Congressional duty and high on the list of public enemies kept by the British, she and baby Peter kept one jump ahead of the redcoated raiding parties. In the running reports she sent her husband, Sally Jay would dramatize little episodes: The neighboring doctor comes in muttering, "Bad news, Mrs. Jay." "Ay, Doctor, what now!" "The [redcoats], madam, are landed at Peekskill."[5] But she would spare the scary details till the danger had passed. In this instance, she then reported those raiders had trashed Governor Livingston's house just moments after she and the baby had escaped.

In the same seemingly lighthearted vein she would also tease brothers and sisters. To her brother Brockholst, then a colonel in the American army, she reports that her husband is away on Congressional duty — "How long it will be before he returns depends upon the limits you army gentlemen prescribe for General Burgoyne"[6] — who, even as she wrote, was barreling down on nearby Albany.

Later, when the Jays went on the mission to Spain and took Brockholst along as private secretary to broaden his education, he turned out to be a terrible trouble-maker. Livingston conspired with the official secretary, William Carmichael, to undercut the whole mission, publicly criticizing Jay for negotiating with the wrong Spaniards, and even at the dinner table ridiculing him before guests from the Spanish government. Sally wrote a detailed report to her father listing Brockholst's crimes but did not send it, only keeping it in reserve in case her brother should have misrepresented the events.[7]

One crime Sally Jay could not let pass, however, was the unpardonable sin Carmichael had committed — interfering with her sending and receiving letters. She called him, "The most insidious and deceitful man" she had ever known. Next to Jay and her babies, letters were her ruling passion, the safety valve for her temper and the proving ground for her wit. Reporting to her mother on the rough voyage to Spain, she tells how the original vessel broke apart in the storm, tossed like an eggshell. That ship, she insisted, could not have stayed steady if they had put it in the stocks.[8]

Her sister Susie congratulated Sally on being the consummate letter-writer: "They say a woman can't write more than two pages without a scandal. You must be more or less than a woman, for you have written 13 pages without a scandal."[9] Clearly letter-writing was her cure for loneliness, though she quipped that she was not so lonely "as to be tired of myself."[10]

She could pass on gossip when appropriate but always with a little bite of Sally Jay wit. When John Jay was being ignored by the Spanish court, she proclaimed her pride in being an American blessed with freedom, then caught herself up: "But wither, my pen, are you hurrying me? What have I to do with politicks? Am I not myself a woman, and writing to Ladies? Come, then, fashions, to my assistance."[11] Even then she fooled around, assuring her sisters that Spanish fashions were the same as last year's American fashions only more expensive.

Aside from the obligatory family news and fun, her preferred topics had to do with politics and diplomacy, keeping both absent Jay and the folks back home up-to-date on current events and affairs. "I have just been interrupted by a visit from the Princess Mazarin, who informed me that the Count d'Artois would be here in 8 or 10 days hence, and the Prince, her husband, soon after."[12] But she does not stop with news. She offers her analysis: "So I conjecture the siege of Gibraltar is to be abandoned."

Living in Paris meant supplying her sisters, especially

sister Kitty who was then staying with the Robert Morrises, all the fashion news. Rumors spread that she so resembled Queen Marie Antoinette that French people would rise when she entered a theatre.[13] She did attend the theatre once when the Queen was present and made herself "almost forgetful of republican principles" in admiring her.[14] What she admired most of all was the Queen's insistence on educating the four-year-old Princess at home — an insistence that Sally Jay found "worth of imitation even by republicans."

The folks back home also expected full reports on the Paris social scene, some details of which had to be pieced together from other correspondents. Benjamin Latrobe recorded this jest at a memorable event in one of Franklin's parties: An American widow in Europe to supervise her son's education in 1781 fancied herself expert in French. At one of Franklin's parties, "his grandson, Temple Franklin, entered the room" kissing the lady nearest the door and then each lady around the room in turn. "Last of all, he kissed Mrs. Jay. Mrs. Jay, unused to such gallantry, blushed so deeply that Dr. Franklin observing it, asked why she blushed. Mrs. M [the American widow] immediately answered, 'Parcequ'il a lui baissé la derrière' — instead of *la dernière*."[15]

Whether founded in fact or not, the jest reflects Sally Jay's reputation as the darling of Franklin's salon, a refreshingly innocent American beauty "unused to such gallantry." The ingenuousness in society masked successively grave responsibilities. With Jay absent in England to recover from exhaustion from negotiating, she took full responsibility for the children. Her report, after the event, of the babies' inoculations is still touching:

Having had the children inoculated without Jay's permission, Mrs. Jay now reported that on the ninth day after the inoculation, baby Anne almost went into convulsions. The maid and the other children were terrified, but Mrs. Jay tried to keep cool, bathing Anne's feet in lukewarm water, keeping her in a cold draft, walking up and down all night in front of the open windows till the fever declined. "In the morning when the Doctor visited me he assured me that all danger was over, and that the measures I had taken prevented her from having convulsions."[16]

Thus the French adventure was not all fun and games. The social experience did, however, prove invaluable when the Jays returned to America. In the confederacy of the times, he was named secretary of foreign affairs which meant de facto head of state, since the president presided only over Congress as a kind of figurehead while the secretary met ambassadors and conducted the country's executive business. This meant that Sally Jay acted as the national First Lady.

The irony was that the President's wife, Mrs. Cyrus Griffin, was an actual Lady in the British aristocracy who had eloped to America before the War. But the lead in New York social life fell to ladylike Sally Jay, now skilled in French society and fashions. Her dinner parties became legendary, her guest lists still a source for studying the history of American manners. They included lawyers and judges, preachers, officers, legislators, and of course ambassadors from the Western world.

Her tact and Jay's diplomacy were truly tested during the season of 1788 with the arrival in New York of a new French envoy, Count de Moustier, who brought along his eccentric sister-in-law Madam la Marquise de Bréhan. The count was a particularly obnoxious character, vain, demanding, and insulting. He called President Cyrus Griffin a tavernkeeper in his own home. He insisted on taking his own chef when he went to dinner at anybody else's house.

His sister-in-law was an eccentric, reportedly "a little, singular, whimsical, hysterical old woman" whose constant companions were a monkey and a little black servant boy.[17] But rumors soon spread that she herself was more than a companion to the count, and more than a sister-in-law. Whether she was in fact his mistress is unclear, but as Jay reported to Jefferson, then ambassador to France, the couple had made themselves so obnoxious to Americans, France had better recall the envoy: "You can easily conceive the influence of such an opinion on the minds and feelings of such a people as ours."[18] France replaced the count within a year.

For the next half-dozen years Mrs. Jay doubled as the nation's party-giver and leader of the New York society and fashions. Her stress on French fashions disturbed some observers who, like Abigail Adams Smith, found she "dresses showily" but even so made a lovely impression. Mrs. Smith, who had also lived in Paris, found that her French dinners "exhibited more of European taste than I expected."[19]

She managed all this even when Jay was appointed chief justice in the new federal government which necessitated his traveling the circuit for three months at a time. His absence compounded her illness. They wrote letters back and forth every day. She concluded hers: "Sick or well, living or dying, I shall remain, my dearest husband, ever yours!" She did try to maintain social rounds with the ladies of the new administration but found Martha Washington stodgy and uninteresting and Elizabeth Hamilton "excessively tedious."[20]

She found herself sharing hostess duties with Mrs. Washington and Mrs. Adams, both of whom disliked parties. The three of them shared official receptions with Mrs. Adams as hostess on Mondays, Mrs. Jay on Tuesdays, and Mrs. Washington on Fridays. She was also their local guide and companion. With widower Jefferson as secretary of state she had also to maintain her role as hostess for foreign dignitaries — all this while carrying the load as leader of New York society. Even after the seat of government moved to Philadelphia she would bear that burden. Distasteful though it may have been, the role was her patriotic duty.

Through the stress and strain she sustained her dual role as father and mother, for, though chief justice, Jay still had to ride the circuit, covering a thousand miles away from home even at Christmas. Besides routine household decisions, she had to decide on where to send the children to school — and continuing decisions on inoculations — asking his concurrence after the fact.

Increasingly declining in health, she was forced to spend weeks at a time in the countryside. Nevertheless, she continued to manage domestic affairs in Jay's absences, collecting debts, investing in stocks, and sending him meticulous records of her transactions that reflected consummate competence in managing the comfortable income he inherited from his family and she from the remnants of the Livingston fortune.

Of the many separations in their twenty-eight-year marriage the one that pained most deeply came about when President Washington sent Jay to London to negotiate still another treaty, the one bearing his name. He took their 18-year-old son Peter along as his secretary just as years before he had taken Sally's brother Brockholst. As in the earlier years she kept in touch by mail but now with more poignancy, less wit. She picks up her pen after a violent storm the night before:

"The poplars this morning were on the ground, and the cherries, still unripe, were blown from the trees before the dining room window into the stable yard. Frank [the servant] has raised the poplars. When *I* droop who shall raise me, if the wide ocean should swallow up my husband and child?"[21]

This particular separation lasted too long. She tried to recapture the wit and humor of earlier letters but now weakened by illness, distracted by too many social obligations, she found it increasingly difficult even to supply the detailed political reports of old. People thought she was interested only in social affairs and preferred to talk politics with her husband. She told her son Peter, "Your father has the advantage — People [want] to give him [political news] but who is interested in me?"[22]

She had played her role of hostess too well. Yet her private concerns for her husband dwelt largely upon politics. Failing to capture the governor's office from the entrenched political machine in New York, Jay regretted only that the office would have meant staying home with his family. For her the regret was compounded. When she heard that brother Brockholst had conspired against her husband, the old temper flared good as new: "Oh," she exclaimed, "how is the name of Livingston to be disgraced! These shameless men, blinded by malice, ambition, and interest . . . ."[23]

In her isolated role, she became more and more impatient with political rumors — "I so frequently hear contradicted one day what has been asserted the preceding that I fear to commit myself by repeating what I do hear."[24] But a quarter-century's routine was hard to break, clearly marking it as rumor or gossip but not taking the trouble to analyze it for her absent husband.

Jay returned with his treaty to find he'd been elected governor at last, and at last the little family could stay together — at least until the state capital moved to Albany. Stepping down after two terms, Jay also turned down President Adams' offer to rename him to the United States Supreme Court so that he could retire to the new home he had built for the whole family in rural Bedford.

Sally Jay said, "I have never enjoyed so much comfort as I do here,"[25] finding at Bedford the serenity that had so far eluded her since they were wed. The Jays had two years of uninterrupted bliss until she died, aged 45, calm of mind, all passion save love spent in the spring of 1802. John Jay would survive another quarter-century solaced by the deeply religious faith that had bound their lives together though apart. Both thought of death as merely another one of those brief separations one suffers — as she had suffered so much else — in the name of duty.

Extracts from Sally Jay's Letters

1777 Parsippany, New Jersey

August 18. [to her brother Henry "Harry" Brockholst
Livingston:] The ravages and destructive cruelties which
appear to be the inevitable lot of poor New York and the
sufferings which many of our hapless friends have already
experienced, together with the more immediate dangers to
which a beloved brother is exposed, are circumstances sufficient to erase from a mind even less susceptible of anxious
forethought the very traces of joy and gaiety that used to mark
my converse and my conduct. May the sad prospect which
we have in view introduce those more useful guests, I mean
fortitude and resignation, which alone can support us in these
changing scenes. . . .

Yesterday Mr. Jay bid us adieu in order to attend the
convention [of the Council of Safety]. How long it will be
before he returns depends upon the limits you army
gentlemen prescribe for General Burgoyne. Is it not a mor-
tification to us who disclaim the tyranny of the King of
England that even the most interesting actions of our lives
are controlled by his minions? . . .

Can you, my dear Harry, pardon me for not telling you
before that when Mr. Jay was at Philadelphia, he had the
felicity of seeing your fair friend, and that he left her in health
and spirits? So I find, my very sly brother, that the reward
you very humbly propose to yourself for all your dangers and
toil is no less than would have been esteemed a sufficient
prize for the victorious arms of either Greece or Troy. [R.B.
Morris, ed., *John Jay: Unpublished Papers* (New York, 1975-80)
1:437-38]

September 3. [to her husband]: No less than three weeks
have already elapsed and not a single line from my beloved
friend. Lord Chesterfield tells his son that women never
frame any excuse arising from business or any other circumstance to apologize for the silence of a correspondent but
always make a point of attributing it to neglect. How much
his lordship was mistaken, I leave you to judge when I assure
you that the suspension of a pleasure which I have frequently

told you was the prime satisfaction I enjoy in your absence is attributed by me to the negligence of some person or other to whom you have entrusted the care of your letters, or perhaps to the want of a safe conveyance, occasioned it may be by your absence from Kingston, and in short to anything but a diminished affection. . . .

I long to know my destination next winter, and yet I could wish not to wait so long as winter neither before your abode is mine. I am the more earnest to be with you upon our son's account. The dear child has been very fractious these two or three weeks, and I know not whether to impute it to ill health or impatience of temper. If the latter be the only cause, I need not tell you how effectually your presence would obviate any difficulty on that score, since his implicit obedience to whatever appeared to be your pleasure is too recent not to be recollected. . . . [R.B. Morris, 1:442-3]

December 12. [to her mother aboard the ship *Confederacy* for Spain]: About four oclock in the morning of the seventh of November, we were alarmed by an unusual noise upon deck, and what particularly surprised me was the lamentations of persons in distress. I called upon the Captain to inform me the cause of this confusion that I imagined to prevail. But my brother desired me to remain perfectly composed, for that he had been upon deck but an half an hour before and left everything in perfect security.

Perfect security! Vain words! don't you think so, mamma? And so indeed they proved. For in that small space of time we had been deprived of nothing less than our bow-spirit, fore-mast, main-mast, and missen-mast so that we were in an awkward situation rendered still more so by a pretty high southeast wind and a very rough sea that prevailed then. However, our misfortunes were only begun. The injury received by our rudder, the next morning, served to complete them as we were ready to conclude.

The groans that distressed me were uttered by two men who had suffered from the fall of the masts. One of them was much bruised, the other had his arm and hand broke. The former recovered, but the latter — poor fellow! — survived not many days the amputation of his arm.

Will it not be painful to my dear mamma to image herself
the situation of her children at that time? Her children, did
I say? Rather let my benevolent mamma imagine the
dangerous situation of more than 300 souls tossed about in
the midst of the ocean in a vessel dismasted and under no
command, at a season too that threatened approaching in-
clemency of weather.

And would you for a moment suppose me capable of
regretting that I had for a time bid adieu to my native land in
order to accompany my beloved friend? Would you have
despaired of ever again embracing your affectionate
children? Or would you have recommended them to Him
who appointed to the waters their bounds; who saith unto the
wave, "Thus far shalt thou go," and to the winds, "Peace, be
still"? Mamma's known piety and fortitude sufficiently suggest the answer to the two latter queries.

And to the former it becomes me to reply, "I do," and
assure you that in no period of our distress, though ever so
alarming, did I once repine, but incited by his amiable example, I gave fear to the winds and cheerfully resigned myself
to the dispensations of the Almighty. . . .

We are now in smooth seas, having the advantage of
trade-winds which blow directly for the Island [Martinique].
Nor are we, if the calculations made are just, more than 220
miles distant from the destined port. Thus, while our
American friends are amusing themselves by a cheerful
fireside, we are sitting under an awning, comforting ourselves
with the expectation of being soon refreshed by some fine
southern fruits.

I expect in a few days to write to papa and the girls from
Martinique, and if what I hear of crabs, fresh fruit, and oysters
be true, I'll make papa's mouth water and make him wish to
forego the pleasure of pruning trees, speechifying assemblies, and what not, for the greater pleasure of messing
with us. [R.B. Morris, 1:680- 2]

1780 Madrid, Spain

August 28. [to her mother reporting the death of new-
born Susan:] On Monday the 22nd day after the birth of my

little innocent, we perceived that she had a fever but were not apprehensive of danger until the next day when it was attended with a fit. On Wednesday the convulsions increased and on Thursday she was the whole day in one continued fit, nor could she close her little eye-lids until Friday morning, the 4th of August at four oclock, when wearied with pain the little sufferer found rest in − −. Excuse my tears − you, too, mamma have wept on similar occasions. Maternal tenderness causes them to flow, and reason, though it moderates distress, cannot entirely restrain our grief, nor do I think it should be wished. ...

But let me not be so rapt in my own feelings as to forget that you, mamma, are not without yours. Doubtless you are solicitous to know the state of my own health, and I am happy that I can gratify your generous curiosity and at the same time give you the pleasure which I know you'll receive from my assurances of my entire recovery. Never was any person more favored by providence than myself during my late confinement, for I not only escaped many disorders incidental to women in childbed, but was even free from the lightest fever and indeed from all kind of pain.

This climate is peculiarly favorable to women in that situation, of which I could tell you instances that are really surprising. But letters are no longer the free medium by which different friends unbosom themselves to each other. Everything therefore that prudence bids us suppress at present, we'll entertain ourselves with when sitting together by an American fireside. You see, mamma, I don't despair of the happiness of seeing you again. ...

Oh! mamma, I never fully comprehended the affection of parents for their children till I became a mother, and never even then was convinced how closely they were twisted with the fibres of the heart until a late painful separation. ... Pappa was disappointed in not receiving a letter from me before I left Philadelphia. It at the same time convinces me of his tenderness and distresses for me having wounded it. But, Oh my dear papa! is it then an easy matter to write a farewell letter at such a time, under such circumstances, and where the heart is so deeply interested?

Had I indulged my own feelings, must not those that were dearer to me than my own been hurt? Had I restrained them, might not I have been supposed insensible? I chose therefore to save us both, to let the idea of business prevail. But I was wrong. No affliction wounds so deeply or lasts so long as neglect, or supposed neglect, from those we love and have obliged.

My mistake was an error of the head, not the heart, for I would rather die than that pappa or mamma should think me capable of ingratitude to them. . . . [R.B. Morris, 1:710-12]

September 1. [to Molly Morris, thanking her for giving refuge to her sister Kitty Livingston while fighting raged near the family homestead:] If I was not myself attached to this little namesake of my friend, I should perhaps be somewhat jealous lest she rival my only son in the affection of his aunt, for Kitty confesses that Maria and Peter are equally dear to her.

How vain, my dear Morris! my efforts to divert my thoughts from grief while my heart is still under its influence for the loss of a lovely little [infant] daughter. The distant train of thought I took to shun this painful subject has, it seems, led me to it. The recollection of your charming little circle renews my sorrow for my own disappointment, since to resemble you in that circumstance, and indeed in every other, would add greatly to my felicity.

But private affections give place to public calamities, they so often agitate my mind as frequently to interrupt my tranquility. The variety of reports circulating here subject me at one time and another to fear, hope, indignation, grief, and in short every emotion of the mind but despair. Far, very far, be that from any of us. My heart recoils with horror from the idea of submission to such ignoble foes.

Sincerely do I sympathize with Mr. Gouverneur Morris on account of that cruel accident [loss of a leg] that has befallen him. If I am not mistaken, that misfortune will call forth latent virtues that will enhance his merit and consequently increase the esteem of which he is already the object. Will you be so obliging as to present my compliments to him? . . . When Mr. Jay returns from San Ildefonso (where the court at present resides) I'll take the liberty of writing again to my dear friend, for then the natural cheerfulness of my disposition will revive and perhaps that letter will partake as much of the spirits which his company never fails to inspire as I am sure this does of the dejection which has been too much indulged in his absence.

Tell me, I beseech you, that you pardon me for this un-amusing letter. New friends are not often sought or desired while strong attachments to the old ones remain. I fear therefore I shall often trouble mine, for to whom but those far distant ones, whom I love, admire and esteem, can I unbosom myself? [HM 13502]

1782, Madrid Spain

June 24. [to her father complaining about her brother Brockholst's meanness, conspiring with Jay's secretary Carmichael — a letter apparently not sent after all — here largely paraphrased:]

After pointing out this is a painful task but necessary for justice to the family's honor, she reports that her brother showed "discontent and disgust" soon after they arrived in Madrid. She knew his "irritible temper" "but I flattered myself that the generosity of disposition which I had remarked with pleasure in our family would secure us from impoliteness except at times when his passions were not under the influence of his reason and which I could readily have pardoned." Mr. Jay's forbearance "even when most insolently treated by him" has outmatched her own.

Two or three times she talked with Jay about it, but he displayed "uncommon meekness," thus making matters worse. "Brockholst's idea of his own importance rose." At a dinner party, he argued for the French custom of drinking wine versus American congressmen's habit of getting drunk after dinner. Sally remarked to Jay later about the imprudence of such remarks in a foreign country, but the next day her brother again criticized Congress before Spanish visitors.

Brockholst, she said, insisted that "the Americans ought to speak their sentiments of Congress with the utmost freedom. . . . There were among them as great rascals as in other assemblies, and that indeed he knew some."

When she retorted, "We should be careful not to lessen" their respectability abroad, Brockholst left for Carmichael's house saying, "There we can say what we please." When he later returned he said that he "preferred going to America to remaining like a slave here."

"Some indecencies in Brockholst's conversation made me quite as angry as himself," she went on, and Jay had to intervene, urging her to compose herself and telling Brockholst to go to bed. As too frequently, Brockholst ridiculed Jay's advice.

Her basic complaint was the way he treated Jay. Jay had been giving him a regular allowance and placed no restrictions on his twenty-four-year-old brother-in-law, who "repaid with hatred." She blamed Carmichael — "Good God, papa, so dearly as we love America! that all our unquiet should proceed from those who received their birth in that favored country."

Carmichael's "cloven foot was not concealed as formerly." His jealousy of Livingston, Senior, caused him to work upon the son, even to influencing Brockholst to divulge confidential information. Brockholst's excuse: "Such caution is all damn nonsense." She said Carmichael is directly responsible for her brother's behaving so rudely to Jay before company "in the most indecent and unprovoked manner."

She concludes by assuring her father of her cheerful disposition in spite of the long distance from her friends, separation from her son, loss of an infant daughter, and distress from a mistaken brother and insincere ex-friend in a foreign land.] [R.B. Morris, 2:188-94]

1782 Paris

November 13. [to Mary White Morris] With what pleasure, my dear madam, do I take up my pen as a substitute for a conversation with you by admitting no other idea to rob me of your image. I enjoy, at least for the moment, the most pleasing delusion.

Yesterday your little sons by passing their holiday with

me made me very happy. Robert so exceedingly resembles Mr. Morris that I feel for him a respect mingled with my love, though at the same time I regret his distance from his father's example and counsel.

When as it sometimes happens among our little Americans that my decision is referred to respecting matters of right and wrong, I always request Robert's opinion; and when he hesitates, I ask him what he thinks would be his father's sentiments upon such occasions − to which he generally replies very justly, and I remark to him the certainty of his acting with propriety while he imitates so worthy an example.

Tommy (who is likewise a fine boy) told me that his last letter mentioned Hetty's and Maria's illness. I hope they are now quite recovered, as well as my dear Kitty. Will you embrace them for me?

If during my stay in Paris it is in my power to serve you, nothing, my dear Mrs. Morris, can give me greater pleasure than receiving of commands. At present the prevailing fashions are very decent and very plain. The gowns most worn are the robes a l'Angloise which are exactly like the Italian habits that were in fashion in America at the time I left it . . . if trimmed, either with [silk] or with gauze, is dress, but if entirely untrimmed must be worn with an apron and is undress. Negligees are very little in vogue; fans of eight or ten sous are almost the only ones in use. . . .

The Queen has lately returned to Versailles after a residence of eight or ten weeks at Passy. While there, I used sometimes to have the pleasure of seeing her at the plays. She is so handsome, and her manners are so engaging that, almost forgetful of republican principles, I was ever ready while in her presence to declare her born to be a queen.

There are, however, many traits in her character worthy of imitation even by republicans, and I cannot but admire her resolution to superintend the education of Madame Royale, her daughter, to whom she has alotted chambers adjoining her own and persists in refusing to name a [governess] for her. The Duchess of Polniac is named for that office to the Dauphin. . . . [HM 13510]

1783 Passy

July 17. [to Mary White Morris, responding to her letter of January 5, 1783:] You do me justice, my dear madam, in believing that the sincere attachment I feel for Mr. Morris and yourself is extended to your children; for permit me to assure you that nothing could afford either Mr. Jay or myself greater pleasure than opportunities of serving them. Indeed, my chagrin at parting with them was heightened by the reflection that I should now be deprived of the pleasure of evincing my friendship for their parents by attentions to them.

Mr. Jay obtained a promise from Robert to write him once a fortnight, but Tommy seemed to think the request rather large as he had other correspondents, and therefore did not positively acquiesce in the proposal, at least as to the frequency. Mr. Ridley [who brought them from America] has already received letters from them expressing their satisfaction with their situation, and I was not a little pleased to find that they still remembered us. They are amiable, sensible boys, and I think promise to repay the tenderness and liberality of their indulgent parents.

I am glad that Mr. Ridley has placed them with a gentleman who was too sensible of the value of freedom to join this aristocratic party in trampling on the liberty of that unfortunate republic [i.e., the boy's tutor, Nicolas de Basseville, of the Dutch Republic]; as by his conversation the sentiments of liberty will be cherished in them in private, while the examples of public tyranny will early impress their minds with the necessity of guarding against the first violation of public freedom.

Thank you, my dear Madam, for your congratulations on the return of Peace, and most sincerely partake your joy in that event, not only on account of the train of blessings that our country will derive from it, but likewise for the flattering prospect it affords me of embracing in a few months my dear Mr. and Mrs. Morris and other amiable friends.

Kitty, you say, intends leaving you soon. How I pity her feelings on that occasion, for though 'tis true that an affectionate mother and sister whom she loves attend with impatience her return to them, yet, where so much gratitude and esteem is due, a sensible heart like hers must melt at separation. How delicately does my dear Mrs. Morris insinuate herself into the hearts of her friends. She knows too well the friend she writes to, to doubt the pleasure she receives from her obliging expressions of regret at parting with her sister.

If your sweet little Maria is grown out of my remembrance, how much must Miss Hetty be altered! Please to embrace them both for me and believe me to be most sincerely attached to you and yours. . . . [HM 13516]

Ann Morris, from an 1810 pastel by James Sharples

ANN RANDOLPH MORRIS

Born Tuckahoe Plantation, Albermarle County, Virginia, July 1774.

Died Morrisania (Bronx), New York, 28 March, 1837.

Fourth of seven girls among 13 children, ten of whom grew to maturity, born to Thomas Mann Randolph, Sr. and Anne Cary Randolph, his second cousin.

Wed Gouverneur Morris 25 December 1809.

One child — Gouverneur Morris, Jr. (1813-1888).

Sister-in-law of Martha Jefferson Randolph.

NANCY MORRIS

On Christmas day 1809, old bachelor Gouverneur Morris, 56, married a spinster half his age, Ann Cary "Nancy" Randolph of the Virginia Randolphs. Their union surprised everybody because he had long been the model confirmed bachelor and prototype jetsetter, while the last half of her life had been as an impoverished gentlewoman, destitute, homeless, trailed by clouds of innuendo, rumor, and scandals of adultery and child-killing.

Those who knew Morris would have joked that this was exactly his taste in women. Brilliant, tall, handsome, wealthy, stylist of the U.S. Constitution, Jefferson's successor in France, model in Paris for Houdon's celebrated statue of

George Washington, he had an international reputation as a lady's man. Popular myth explained his wooden leg came from jumping out a bedroom window to avoid an irate husband. In fact, he broke it leaping for his moving carriage like a modern cowboy mounting his horse at breakneck speed.[1] Physicians cut off the leg. John Jay quipped that Morris would have settled down if they had cut off a different limb.[2]

When Morris, with no forethought of matrimony, had asked Nancy Randolph to be his housekeeper at Morrisania (now the Bronx, New York), her first response was conditioned by his notoriety. She warned him that she would stand for no hanky-panky. He was perfectly honest with her, conceding that while age may have cooled his heat somewhat, the rashness of youth still sometimes broke out. "I can only answer that I will love you as little as I can."[3]

On her part, she insisted on telling him about the scandals that had made her life miserable since, as an impressionable 17-year-old given to romantic novels, she had fallen in love with a 20-year-old cousin who could not marry her — not because he was a cousin, for the Randolphs usually married cousins, but because of two other factors: Her father forbade the marriage on financial grounds, and her lover died of tuberculosis at 21.

From their union, however, apparently came a child; whether stillborn or murdered remains unresolved — even whether there was a child at all. In scandals of 1793 she had kept silent as Hester in *The Scarlet Letter*, not even disclosing the name of the putative child's father so that some were led to believe it had not been her lover but his brother — a more gruesome bit, since that brother was married to her sister and she lived with them.

She did nothing to dispel even that rumor, no doubt to protect the Randolph name. In 1815, when the scandals surfaced, impelled by evil, she told her sad tale publicly to protect both name and fortune of her adorable 2-year-old Gouverneur Morris, Jr.

Even so, all the facts are not known. The event responsible for the scandal can only be reconstructed out of her public statements and from depositions from folks on the scene who would disagree on even such simple questions as whether she looked pregnant in what must have been at least her eighth month. The outlines seem clear enough to summarize.

The year was 1792; Nancy's beloved mother had died three years earlier. Her father had married again, a young woman not much older than Nancy. Friction was inevitable, and so Nancy spent as much time as she could visiting her married brothers or sisters. On the last night of September, she had been staying with sister Judy and her husband Richard Randolph. With a group of other young cousins they were visiting a neighboring plantation. They were awakened in the night by Nancy's shrieking in pain.

Richard, along with a couple of young servant girls, tried to help with laudanum, an opium solution, while Judy kept the others away by explaining that Nancy frequently suffered painful periods. Everyone seemed satisfied with that explanation until within a few days the slaves started passing on rumors that Nancy had given birth to a child which Richard had carried out and flung on the woodpile — although no corpse was ever found.

The rumors took on more sordid details as they spread across Virginia and beyond. Now it was said that Richard, rather than his deceased brother Theodoric, had fathered the child and maintained adultery under the very nose of Judy.

Hoping to put an end to the gossip, Richard put an advertisement in the *Virginia Gazette* challenging anybody to file a legal accusation so that a court could judge on the truth — otherwise he would turn himself in for a judicial hearing.[4] A panel of a dozen magistrates looked at the charges and threw them out of court without going to trial.

Both Richard and Judy gave their sides of the story to the public through advertising. By keeping silent, Nancy only piqued the curiosity of the gossips, especially when she went on living with the couple at their plantation, "Bizarre," for the next ten years.

At Richard's death, Judy's affairs became managed by his remaining brother, John Randolph of Roanoke. A childhood disease had unsexed him. His compensation was making the lives around him as miserable as his own. Mad, irascible, brilliant, devious, he badgered Nancy into leaving "Bizarre," turning her out destitute and homeless, dependent on the charity of friends in Richmond.

In the first flush of independence, with a little money from her own brother, she could imperiously reject Randolph's gift of $100. With time, however, she would ask him for loans just to survive. Drifting northward she lived in Newport, Rhode Island, then found a teaching position at a new academy in Stratford, Connecticut, near New York. It was in New York that Morris rediscovered her.

He had known her many years earlier when he would visit her father on business and see 14-year-old Nancy racing her pony across the fields against the wind. Now in 1808 he asked a favor for old times' sake. He needed help managing his estate, Morrisania, and asked her to serve as gentlewoman-housekeeper to keep the servants in line.

Her first response was to question the propriety of a spinster coming to live in the same house with a notorious rogue. He replied in kind, noting that none of his previous housekeepers had been called immoral — "I can only say that our real relations shall be that of friends."[5] And when she insisted on telling him about the scandal that had dogged her these long years, he told her, "If we ever happen to be alone you shall tell your tale of sorrow when the tear from your cheek may fall on my bosom."[6] He, too, knew the language of romantic novels.

She went as housekeeper to Morrisania in April 1809 and on Christmas Day married Morris. To show that she was not marrying him for money, she insisted on being married in one of the two gowns she owned — both patched at the elbows.[7] And to show that his intentions were more than honorable he presented her with a most handsome prenuptial contract allaying her fears of ever being homeless again.

Morris's relatives who stood to inherit his estate made no secret of their panic. They protested the folly of this old bachelor marrying a spinster half his age — hardly the stuff a public conditioned by romantic novels would take seriously. He replied with typical Morrisanian wit: "If the world were to live with my wife, I should certainly have consulted its taste." Since it was he who would live with her, he had consulted nobody else's taste but his own.[8]

Their marriage seemed truly made in heaven. Nancy accompanied him on his official tour as commissioner for developing the Erie Canal. This meant taking a sort of unofficial honeymoon at Niagara Falls, through northern New York, down the Mohawk Trail to Washington for congressional hearings. Inseparable, they made a delightful couple. It was as if Nancy had come through her lifetime of misery unscathed.

During the misery years, friends were constantly astonished that she could laugh at herself. In one letter, she recalled how a friend of her youth characterized her during those dark days: "Someone asked Madame Yrujo if I retained my vivacity unimpaired. 'Oh heavens!' she exclaimed, 'the most serious moralist of the age.'"[9] Now in the moment of ultimate happiness that affability would be truly tested.

Her baby came on 9 February 1813. The effect on the other Morris heirs can be imagined. One potential heir nicknamed the child after the then famous Russian General Kutusov. The other heirs reacted with more venom, casting about for some means of discrediting Nancy and thereby disinheriting Gouverneur Morris, Jr. The instrument turned up as Nancy's earlier nemesis, John Randolph of Roanoke, who had turned her out of sister Judy's home. The conspirators now led him to believe that Nancy had poisoned Judy's husband, his brother Richard.

They encouraged him to write a vicious exposé addressed to Morris accusing her directly of that foul crime while reminding him about the child murder of October 1792. The excuse for this letter, datelined Halloween 1814, was to prevent her from working her wiles on Morris — keeping him a prisoner in his own home, driving away friends and loyal servants who might expose the sex orgies going on under his very nose.

Randolph went further, accusing her of intending to kill Morris as she had killed Richard, only this time taking both

Morris and the child abroad where she could operate more easily — abandoning him and the baby on the highway. He reminded her of the precedent in child-killing when Richard's "hands received the burthen, bloody from the womb, and already lifeless. Who stifled its cries, God only knows and you."[10]

That was only the warmup. Randolph went on to remind her that she had lived in adultery with Richard before poisoning him, but even so Judy had forgiven her and allowed her to remain at Bizarre until Nancy had committed the ultimate sin of becoming concubine of her household slave, "dear Billy Ellis." That, insisted Randolph, was why Judy had to send her sister out into the cold, destitute and homeless, and into the life of a "drab."[11] He, too, had read romantic novels. "What do I see?" he wound up. "A vampire that, after sucking the blood of my race, has flitted off to the North and struck her harpy fangs into an infirm old man." The real reason for writing, he insisted, was to warn Morris: "If he be not blind and deaf he must sooner or later unmask you unless *he too die of cramps*," like poor Richard.

But Morris's reaction was coolness itself: "Mr. Randolph's communication gave me no concern, for Mrs. Morris had apprised me of the only fact in his possession" (no doubt the "lifeless" still birth) "before she came to my house, so that her candor had blunted the point of his arrow."[12]

Nancy's candor now boiled over into public confession. She composed a 4000-word reply — which Randolph claimed he never did receive — then, together with certified copies of Randolph's own letter, sent at least 6 copies of hers to friends in Virginia and indeed to anyone who asked for copies. Within three months copies were circulating so widely as to make biographer William Cabell Bruce speculate whether "any unprinted thing of the kind has ever been so frequently copied and circulated."[13]

The letter is really a justification of her own ways as a headstrong heiress of an impoverished Randolph family whose error was in loving not wisely but too well. As that sin was marked by the death of one child, so the expiation after years of suffering was marked by the birth of a marvelous boy.

The part of Satan was played by John Randolph of Roanoke. "That your brother Theodoric paid his addresses to me, you knew and attempted to supplant him by calumny.... You hoped it was not true, for he was unworthy of me. To establish this opinion, you made many assertions derogatory to his reputation — some of which I knew to be false." The effect was contrary to what he intended and helped her decide to rebel against her father's wishes.

"Under these circumstances, I was left at Bizarre, a girl, not seventeen, with the man she loved. I was betrothed to him, and considered him as my husband in the presence of [God]. We should have been married, if Death had not snatched him away a few days after the scene which began the history of my sorrows" — the consummation of their love. (Consulting gynecologist for this study, Richard D. Pettit, M.D., points out that Theodoric's tuberculosis would have increased his sex drive even as he lay dying.)

Naturally Nancy said nothing about that but went on to review the way she and Richard were persecuted for child killing "in a remote county of Virginia more than twenty years ago. You have revived the slanderous tale in the most populous city in the United States," and she did not intend to sit idly by this time.

"You have denied the fact of turning me out of doors." Her memory said otherwise: "You came into my room one evening, after you had been a long time in your chamber with my sister, and said, addressing yourself to me, 'Nancy, when do you leave this house? The sooner the better for you take as many liberties as if you were in a tavern.'

"On this occasion, as on others, my course was silent submission. I was poor, I was dependent. I knew the house was kept in part at your expense. I could not therefore appeal to my sister. I replied with the humility suitable to my forlorn condition, 'I will go as soon as I can.' You stalked haughtily about the room" — and, then, as if writing a romantic novel of her own with herself playing heroine, she added: "And poor, unprotected 'Nancy' retired to seek the relief of tears."

Banished to an impoverished-gentlewomanly lodging in Richmond, which Randolph had implied was a bawdy house, she began her desperate years battling her pride. She remonstrated against his turning her out of doors as a troublemaker. "I was continually occupied at my needle or other work for the house, obeying, to the best of my knowledge, the orders I received, differing from any other servant only in this: I received no wages but was permitted to sit at table, where I did not presume to enter into conversation or taste of wine, and very seldom of tea or coffee."

Then she recollected the only time he had visited her during all those years: "You sat on my bedstead, I cannot say my bed, for I had none, I was too poor. When weary, my limbs were rested on a blanket spread over the sacking." The result was an offer of a hundred dollars as from her sister Judy, but her Randolphian pride resisted. "My feelings were too indignant to receive a boon at the hand of those by whom I had been so grievously wounded."

In later years, when being hungry and homeless had worn that pride thin, she had asked for a loan of half that sum: "Afterwards, when in Newport, suffering from want and borne down by a severe ague and fever, I was so far humbled as to request not the gift (I would sooner have perished) but the loan of half that sum. My petition struck on a cold heart that emitted no sound."

Her subsequent marriage caused great anxiety among Morris's heirs but nothing like that caused by the birth of Gouverneur Morris, Jr. The exchange of letters between Randolph and Nancy is thus less a Randolph family feud than an attempt on her part to protect the baby's estate. This becomes clear after Morris's death in November 1816 (from trying to open his clogged urethra with a whalebone).[14]

In looking over his diary, Nancy the widow added a woeful note: "I have traced the sufferings of your mind from the first detection of David Ogden's villainy."[15] Grand-nephew Ogden had been trying a little double dealing on loans from Morris. For that, Nancy now took him to court and in the course of litigation showed that it was he who had scripted the scenario of lies in John Randolph's awful letter.[16] Thus her reply was the natural reaction of a mother protecting her young.

She devoted the rest of her life, another twenty years, to Gouverneur Morris, Jr. The original marriage settlement provided her $2600 a year plus Morrisania.[17] Even had she remarried, she would have retained that plus another $600 for added expenses. But she managed the estate so prudently that when he turned 18, a growing replica of his dad — a strapping six-footer — she could celebrate the news that his estate was entirely cleared of debt.[18]

When she died in May 1837, aged 63, the line of Gouverneur Morris was secure. The last of that line, their great-grandson, died in August 1953, a banker in Gallup, New Mexico[19] but who in the early years of this century was a widely known writer of romantic novels his great-grandma would have loved.

Autobiographical Passages From Nancy Morris' Long Letter to John Randolph of Roanoke, 16 January 1815

That your brother Theodoric paid his advances to me, you knew and attempted to supplant him by calumny. Be pleased to remember that in my sister Mary's house, you led me to the portico and, leaning against one of the pillars, expressed your surprise at having heard from your brother Richard that I was engaged to marry his brother, Theodoric. That you hoped it was not true, for he was unworthy of me. To establish this opinion, you made many assertions derogatory to his reputation — some of which I knew to be false. . . .

It was your troublesome attention which induced Richard to inform you of my engagement. At that time my father had other views. Your property, as well as that of your brothers, was hampered by a British debt. My father, therefore, preferred for my husband a person of clear and considerable estate. The sentiment of my heart did not accord with his intentions.

Under these circumstances, I was left at Bizarre, a girl, not seventeen, with the man she loved. I was betrothed to him and considered him as my husband in the presence of that God whose name you presume to invoke on occasions the most trivial and for purposes most malevolent. We should have been married if death had not snatched him away a few days after the scene which began the history of my sorrows.

Your brother Richard knew every circumstance, but you are mistaken in supposing I exacted from him a promise of secrecy. He was a man of honor. Neither the foul imputations against us both, circulated by that kind of friendship which you have shown to my husband, nor the awful scene to which he was afterwards called as an accomplice in the horrible crime with which you attempt to blacken his memory could induce him to betray the sister of his wife, the wife of his brother. I repeat it, sir, the crime with which you now attempt to blacken his memory. . . .

You not only charge me with the heinous crime of infanticide, placing him in the condition of an accomplice, but you proceed to say that "had it not been for the prudence of Mr. Harrison, or the mismanagement of not putting *me* first on my trial, we should both have swung on the same gibbet and the foul stain of incest and murder been stamped on his memory and associated with the idea of his offspring." . . . Who is there of nerve so strong as not to shudder at your savage regret that we did not swing on the same gibbet?

On the melancholy occasion you have thought proper to bring forward there was the strictest examination. Neither your brother or myself had done anything to excite enmity, yet we were subjected to an unpitying persecution. The severest scrutiny took place. You know it. He was acquitted to the joy of numerous spectators, expressed in shouts of exultation. This, sir, passed in a remote county of Virginia more than twenty years ago. You have revived the slanderous tale in the most populous city in the United States.

For what? To repay my kindness to your nephew by tearing me from the arms of my husband and blasting the prospects of my child! Poor innocent babe, now playing at my feet, unconscious of his mother's wrongs. But it seems that on my apprehensions for his life first flashed conviction on your mind that my own hand had deprived in October 1792 that of which I was delivered. You ought to have said, the last of September. . . .

With the same insensibility to shame, which marks your allegations, you have denied the fact of turning me out of doors. This also must be made known in the neighborhood where it must be well remembered. I take the liberty again to refresh your memory. Shortly after your nephew (whom I had nursed several weeks in a dangerous illness at the hazard of my life) had left home to take the benefit of a change in air, you came into my room one evening, after you had been a long time in your chamber with my sister, and said, addressing yourself to me, "Nancy, when do you leave this house? The sooner the better, for you take as many liberties as if you were in a tavern."

On this occasion, as on others, my course was silent submission. I was poor, I was dependent. I knew the house was kept in part at your expense. I could not therefore appeal to my sister. I replied with the humility suitable to my forlorn condition, "I will go as soon as I can." You stalked haughtily about the room, and poor, unprotected Nancy retired to seek the relief of tears. . . .

I must notice another malicious falsehood respecting my residence, while at Richmond. You say I took lodgings at Prior's, a public garden. It is true Mr. Prior owned a large lot in Richmond, and that there was a public building on it, in which public balls and entertainments were given, and this lot a public garden. But it is equally true that Mr. Prior's dwelling and the enclosure round it were wholly distinct from that garden. In that house I lodged.

My chamber was directly over Mrs. Prior's, a lady of as good birth as Mr. John Randolph and of far more correct principles. All this, sir, you perfectly well know. From that chamber, I wrote you a note, complaining that your nephew, then a schoolboy in Richmond, was not permitted to see me. You sent it back, after writing on the same sheet, "I return your note that you may compare it with my answer, and ask yourself if you are not unjust to one who through your life has been your friend."

This, with the recital of your professions of regard made to my friend Lucy Randolph and her husband and her husband's brother Ryland, led me to suppose you had, in the last scene at Bizarre, acted only as my sister's agent. I therefore wrote to you, remonstrating against the reason assigned for turning me out of doors, which you yourself knew to be unfounded, for you had often observed that I was . . . "the Silent Woman."

You knew that I was continually occupied at my needle or other work for the house, obeying to the best of my knowledge the orders I received, differing from any other servant only in this: I received no wages but was permitted to sit at table, where I did not presume to enter into conversation or taste of wine and, very seldom, of tea or coffee. . . .

I pause here, sir, to ask whether, on receipt of this letter, you pretended to deny having turned me out of doors? You dare not say so.

You shortly after paid me a visit, the only one during your stay. You sat on my bedstead, I cannot say my bed, for I had none, I was too poor. When weary, my limbs rested on a blanket spread over the sacking. Your visit was long, and I never saw you from that day until we met in Washington. Some days after, you sent your nephew to offer me $100 on the part of his mother. I supposed this to be a turn of delicacy, for had you been the bearer of money from her, you would have delivered it when you were in my chamber and given me every needful assurance of the quarter from which it came. But let it come from whom it might, my feelings were too indignant to receive a boon at the hands of those by whom I had been so grievously wounded.

I readily conceive, sir, that this must have appeared to you inexplicable, for it must be very difficult for you to conceive how a person in my condition would refuse money from any quarter. It is true that, afterwards, when in Newport, I suffered from want and borne down by a severe ague and fever, I was so far humbled as to request not the gift (I would sooner have perished) but the load of half that sum.

My petition struck on a cold heart that emitted no sound. You did not deign to reply. You even made a boast of your silence. I was then so far off, my groans could not be heard in Virginia. You no longer apprehended the reproaches which prompted your ostentatious offer at Richmond. Yes, sir, you were silent. . . . Yes sir, you were silent. Perhaps you hoped that the poor forlorn creature you had turned out of doors would, under the pressure of want and far removed from every friend, to be driven to a vicious course and enable you to justify your barbarity by charges such as you have now invented. . . .

I have a letter from my sister telling me the pleasure [her son] St. George manifested at the present of my portrait I made him. I have a letter also from her, shortly after her house was burnt, in which she tells me among the few things saved she was rejoiced to find my portrait which you brought out with your own. By this act, you have some right to it and, should my present ill health lead me shortly to the grave, you may hang it up in your castle at Roanoke next to the

Englishman's scalp — a trophy of family prowess.

I observe, sir, in the course of your letter allusion to one of Shakespeare's best tragedies. I trust you are by this time convinced that you have clumsily performed the part of "honest Iago." Happily for my life and for my husband's peace, you did not find him in a headlong, rash Othello. For a full and proper description of what you have written and spoken on this occasion, I refer you to the same admirable author. He will tell you it is a tale told by an idiot, full of sound and fury, signifying nothing. [William Cabell Bruce, *John Randolph* (New York, 1922) 2:278-95]

Morrisania 1815

January 29. [to William B. Giles, transmitting her letter for circulation:] In the morning of life I was impressed with an excellent opinion, not only of your understanding but of your amiable disposition also. The liberty I am about to take is painful in the extreme. Your goodness will, I hope, excuse it.

Mr. Randolph's unprovoked attack on me commenced when I was borne down with the fatigue of nursing his nephew who was continually relapsing and who during a long illness received from his uncle "boasts of heraldry" instead of the assistance he wanted. When we all parted, I believed each member of that family bound to me forever, such had been my exertions to save that suffering young man.

I shall be much obliged to you to forward my answer to Mr. Randolph's letter and keep the certified copy of his until I can find leisure (from the care of my lovely son) to make another copy of my reply, which I shall beg the favor of you to enclose with it to your old acquaintance and friend Mrs. Carrington. [Huntington manuscript BR Box 3 (13)]

1828, Morrisania

May 30. [to Joseph C. Cabell] More than 22 years have elapsed . . . since I came here to live, and I have nothing to reproach myself with. In my husband's biography will be seen an account of his domestic happiness. I knew Mr. Morris in the years 86 and 88. He visited me at old Mrs.

Pollack's in New York in 1808 and expressed a wish that some reduced gentlewoman would undertake to keep his house, as the lower class of housekeepers often provoked the servants to a riot in his dwelling.

He went to his lands where he remained six months. On his return he proposed my coming to keep house for him. I thought it much better to have employment than remain a burthen on my friends. . . . I glory in stating that I was married in a gown patched at the elbows, being one of the only two I had in the world. [Bruce, *John Randolph* 2:300]

Martha Jefferson, from the picture by T. Sully

MARTHA JEFFERSON RANDOLPH

Born Monticello, Virginia, 27 September 1772.

Died of stroke, Edgehill (near Monticello), 10 October 1836.

Eldest of three daughters who survived infancy out of six children born to Thomas and Martha Wayles Skelton Jefferson.

Wed Thomas Mann Randolph, 23 February 1790.

Twelve children — Anne Cary (1791-1826), Thomas (1792-1875), Ellen (1794-95), Ellen Wayles (1796-1876), Cornelia (1799-1871), Virginia (1801-1882), Mary (1803-1876), James Madison (1806-1834), Benjamin Franklin (1808-1871), Meriwether Lewis (1810-1837), Septimia Anne (1814-1887), and George Wythe (1818-1867).

At the White House a few weeks in 1802-03 and 1805-06.

MARTHA JEFFERSON RANDOLPH

When Martha Jefferson turned eleven, her father joked about the way he was bringing her up. With free access to the books at Monticello she would, he wagered, be smarter than any man she married. He figured the odds at "about 14-to-1" that she would marry a blockhead and that she would end up educating their children alone.[1] He turned out to be half right.

Her mother's death at not quite 34 left Thomas Jefferson committed to celibacy ever after. He determined to raise their three daughters, Martha, younger Mary, and baby Lucy as a single parent. No woman could have filled the vacuum left by the death of their mother.

They had wed when he was 29 and she a widow at 23, their romance legendary in Southern story.[2] Right after the ceremony at her father's house they had dashed for Monticello 100 miles away. Snow made no obstacle until drifts three feet high forced them to trade carriage for horseback during the final eight miles.

Arrived at unfinished Monticello, they found the servants asleep, not expecting them to travel during that blizzard. No fire, no light, nothing to eat, he built up a fire himself, found a half-jug of wine in an unfinished bookcase, and lit up the night with song, laughter, and passionate love to last a lifetime.

Lovely — multitalented with all the social graces and the practical and classical wisdom to make her Jefferson's ideal — Martha Wayles Skelton Jefferson had served as business manager for her father, a job she now assumed for Jefferson, freeing him to pursue virtuosi experiments and a public service career that would span 40 years.

A popular woman who loved parties and dancing, she willingly left them behind to play the roles of business manager, wife and mother. She nurtured six children, of whom three were surviving by the time of her own death; also six nieces and nephews bereft of their father, who had been Jefferson's best friend, plus a family of 187 slaves which made her "practically the busiest slave" of all.[3]

Almost perennial pregnancies sapped her delicate frame, so much so that anxiety for her health forced Jefferson to arrive late to the crucial congress of 1776. Nevertheless, she marshaled what strength she had to do her own share for the ensuing war effort.

At Martha Washington's appeal, she headed the Virginia

branch of the Ladies Association, raising money and making clothing for the troops at a time when Congress could supply neither. The Philadelphia branch had pioneered, with Rachel Wilson alone going door-to-door, daring to enter even filthy ale houses, raising a record $64,561.50.[4]

Mrs. Jefferson in her weakened condition could not emulate that kind of solicitation. Taking a leaf from her husband's book, she sent a letter to the local newspaper, the *Virginia Gazette* (9 August 1780), reprinting a letter from one of the Philadelphia ladies. That letter raised fears of infants being snatched from mothers' breasts by the "ferocious enemy," without our brave soldiers to protect them.

Mrs. Jefferson issued an appeal to pity and terror of her own, reminding Virginia mothers that the British and Indians had been massacring settlers along New York's western frontier. Donations, she said, would assist "those brave men who are shielding us from the sword of the one and the scalping knife of the other."

How much of the threat was real, how much imagined? The British did raid Monticello, only to find that Jefferson had ordered the family to shelter elsewhere. He himself hid with his official papers on a neighboring mountain top where he could keep an eye on what was happening below. But the fact of his failing to stay and defend the land scandalized chivalric Virginians, who never let him forget it ever after.

Some folks thought this was the reason he declined a third term as Governor. The real reason was the vow he had made to Mrs. Jefferson never to leave her side again.[5] He remained at home, writing his book, *Notes on Virginia*, educating the little girls, and nursing Mrs. Jefferson as she lay dying from her last childbirth.

Her deathbed scene, recalled by servants, included her direct request that he not marry again. Listing her dying wishes, she embraced the children gathered around the bed, "and spreading out her four fingers she told him she could not die happy if she thought her four children were ever to have a stepmother."[6] Someone misremembered. She had only three children when she died.

Servantlore also has it that Jefferson held her other hand

in his hands and "promised her solemnly that he would never marry again." With that, Martha Wayles Skelton Jefferson died quietly at quarter-to-noon 7 September 1782, aged 33. For weeks after, isolated, inconsolable Jefferson remained, in his own words, "as dead to the world as she was."[7]

Ten-year-old Martha sought to console her father. She never forgot his grief: "He kept his room for three weeks," she recalled, "and I was never a moment from his side. He walked incessantly almost every night and day" and when he did leave the room he would just as incessantly ride his horse, "rambling about the mountain in the least frequented roads just as often through the woods."[8]

Jefferson's sister, other relatives, and plenty of servants looked after four-year-old Mary and the infant Lucy whose birth had brought her mother's death, and who would herself die a torturous death two years later from whooping cough. Jefferson, determined to remain a single parent, took Martha with him to Congress in Philadelphia and then on his mission to Paris.

The 15-year-old's letter back to friends in Philadelphia shows she was her father's girl, with a keen eye for detail. She describes the cabin of the boat taking them across the English Channel as "not more than three feet wide and about four long . . . . The door by which we came in at was so little that one was obliged to enter on all-fours."[9]

She also shared her father's eye for absurdity. When he was away from Paris, she sent him live, local news about a citizen who had just killed himself because his wife did not love him anymore. Martha commented that if every Parisian did the same, the city would be left with nothing but widows.[10]

Jefferson sent her to the best convent school in town, so fashionable that its clientele included aristocracy from Great Britain. But at first Martha faced a language barrier: "I did not speak a word of French," she reported to Philadelphia friends, "and no one here knew English but a little girl of two years old that could hardly speak French." With a little help from new school chums, she learned "very soon," and her letters to the States filled with French idioms.[11]

Death of baby Lucy in October 1784 drove Jefferson once more into deep depression. He sent directly for his remaining little girl, nine-year-old Mary, placing her in the convent school with Martha where she had much less trouble picking up the language, quickly learning to speak French and reading it "as well as English."[12]

She was not, however, as much interested in reading as Martha was. Both girls were shy by nature, but Mary became the school pet and with her sister easily acquired the social graces then fashionable in Europe. In fact, Martha became so expert in saying what was expected of her that Jefferson was shocked to hear she wished to convert to Catholicism. She confessed, however, that she was merely trying to be nice to the convent priest by letting the priest think so.[13]

By the time they returned to America in November 1789, the French Revolution had ravaged Paris. One measure of the girls' concern was Martha's description of the parade that had brought the King back from Versailles in the critical period before the mob became sovereign. She viewed the parade from an upper window. A cry like "bellowings of thousands of bulls" rose from the mob — not for the King but for Lafayette.[14] The highlight for her was the hero's bowing to *her* in front of her pals.

Some of the culture shock of returning after five years abroad must have been relieved by the triumphal return to Monticello, another family legend. This is Martha's granddaughter's version:[15] "The old and young came — women and children — growing impatient, they sauntered down the mountainside and down the road until they met the carriage-and-four at Shadwell (four miles distant) when the welkin rang with their shouts of welcome....

"The horses were actually unhitched, and the vehicle drawn by the strong black arms up to the foot of the lawn in front of the door at Monticello." There the family of slaves made a path for the tall, stately, seventeen-year-old Martha, looking more regal than a princess, and slighter but far more lovely eleven-year-old Mary, now called Maria in the French style, whose delicate loveliness reminded everyone of her mother.

Just a few months later, Martha married Thomas Mann Randolph. The young couple arranged the early wedding to accommodate Jefferson's plans to join the new government in Washington. Other than as an early childhood acquaintance, Martha hardly knew her 22 year-old husband nor he his 18-year-old bride. But the new Secretary of State needed to be in Washington the first of March and so their courtship lasted a hasty four months, a haste both would have reason to regret.

Randolph, of an old but eccentric family, had only just returned from four years at the University of Edinburgh — in those days as good a university as Britain could offer. Martha of course enjoyed the finest education Europe could offer a woman. Her schooling made her even more knowledgeable than her sainted mother had been in music, art, and the classics, but neither of the newlyweds had been prepared for running a Virginia farm — much less a plantation.

Just as the Jeffersons had begun their romantic marriage deeply in debt incurred by Mrs. Jefferson's father, so the newlyweds began theirs in debt because Mr. Randolph, Senior had just wed a new wife and left son Thomas to his own devices. They lived at Monticello the first year. Even from a home of their own, Martha assured her father, "My happiness can never be compleat without your company."[16] Always broke himself, company was all Jefferson could offer, with their returning to Monticello whenever he could break away from Washington.

Maria, despite being the image of her mother, resigned herself to second place in his affections. She said of Martha: "The more I see of her the more I am sensible how much more deserving she is of you than I am; but, my dear papa, suffer me to tell you that the love, the gratitude she has for you could never surpass mine."[17]

Poor Maria, who had wed her cousin John Wayles Eppes in 1797, died like her mother in childbirth. She died in 1804 at 26, having had three babies, only one of whom survived. Even the little girl whose birth killed her died at age 3. By contrast, Martha Randolph presented Jefferson a new grandchild almost every two years from 1791-1818, the last when she was age 46. (Her James Madison Randolph was the first baby born in the White House 17 January 1806).

That artful observer Dolley Madison thought pregnancy became tall, angular Mrs. Randolph. Pregnancy, said Mrs. Madison, left her "fat and cheerful."[18] With her reddish hair, she came more and more to resemble her father. At Maria's death, he had lamented, "My evening prospects now hang on the slender thread of a single life" — Martha's.[19] Hardly likely with several toddling grandchildren always underfoot at Monticello or the White House.

The Randolphs finally made it to a place of their own only five miles from Monticello. Oddly this proved no great advantage. Jefferson's policy of perpetual open house meant that unless she got there before or after the crowds, Martha had slight chance of enjoying his company alone. Worse, she found herself for that reason growing more and more averse to company. To compensate, she devoted herself entirely to the education of her children[20] — just as Jefferson had jokingly prophesied twenty years earlier.

This is not to say that Jefferson neglected the Randolphs. On the contrary, he contrived to spend every summer with them at Monticello while President, and he had Martha and the children with him at the White House for two seasons. It became a source of worldwide amusement when such travelers as the great Von Humboldt reported finding Jefferson roughhousing on the floor with a pack of grandchildren or running races on the back lawn.[21] When not at Monticello, he would counsel Martha by mail on bringing up babies and the conduct of life.

As Martha's brood increased, her marriage seemed to disintegrate. Thomas Randolph had low esteem to begin with, browbeaten by a brutal father, then awed by an idolized father-in-law, how could he have found happiness married to a daughter of Jefferson? The nadir came when Jefferson pointedly excluded him from his will. Jefferson's intent, good lawyer that he was, seems to have been to prevent Randolph's creditors from seizing Martha's portion.

Randolph then abandoned the family and Monticello.

The last ten years of his life he served in the legislature and as a two-term governor of Virginia. He was not the "block-head" Jefferson had prophesied Martha would marry. But after his father-in-law's death, Randolph returned to Monticello, in his own words, "desolate, destitute, isolated and aged" - at 60 "a silly bird among swans."[22]

Martha, by this time spending summers with her daughter Ellen Coolidge in Boston, returned to be with him. Randolph insisted on living apart in the north pavilion with only a stable for his horse, a little plot for a garden, and enough wood for a comfortable fire in winter. He outlived his father-in-law by only two years, and they buried poor Randolph in the family plot at Jefferson's feet.

The passing of her father radically altered Martha Randolph's life. When apart he had written voluminously on national and international affairs — always sent as for her husband's information. She would return news of regional politics and gossip as she could. When he had complained of her not writing, she explained, "I write amidst the noise and confusion of six children interrupted every moment by their questions and so much disturbed by their prattling around me that I catch myself repeatedly writing their words instead of my own thoughts."[23] She knew how to disarm a grandfather.

But Jefferson died so hopelessly in debt that his last years were secretly funded by friends. Monticello was sold at his death. Family friends coming to console her found Martha seated midst rooms stripped to the walls by creditors — no pictures, statues, furnishing, furniture, without a chair to sit on. A year later, staying at a neighboring house with a view of Monticello across the fields, she was found sleeping on the one piece of furniture she had salvaged, Jefferson's old bed, wrapped in his old coverlet.[24]

Randolph's death compounded her misery in that she was now the support of four daughters and four sons, the youngest 12, the eldest with daughters of his own. In addition were a son-in-law still a law student and the aged grandmother he brought with him. Martha kept hoping that Congress would one day repay a loan her father had once made, but realized that the burden of earning a living was now hers.

"I was educated as the heiress of a great estate," she realized, "and was learning music, etc. etc. when I ought to have been acquiring dexterity with my needle."[25] But she also realized that no expert management could have saved Monticello and so did not sorrow on that score but rather turned to the one asset that remained, her education.

On the verge of opening a school, however, she was saved by word that the South Carolina legislature and then the Louisiana legislature had voted her annuities that would see her through — if not in elegance, at least in comfort. So now with a little income and frequent visits to married children she relaxed into a dignified old age, honored by presidents and foreign visitors as Jefferson's daughter.

Attention from Andrew Jackson and Martin Van Buren could have put her at the head of Washington society, but she retained her youthful shyness. At a reception for English author Harriet Martineau, though seated next to her, she said not a word because the touch of Miss Martineau's speaking trumpet made her mind a blank. She also retained her sense of humor. Asked how she liked an oratorio, she replied, "If you ask me about the music I must answer you by a quotation from old Alberti." Alberti, asked how he liked the music of hounds in full cry after a fox, had sighed, "De damn dog make such a noise, me no hear de music."[26]

She died of a stroke aged 64. On her deathbed she clasped a verse her father had composed for her as he lay dying:

A Deathbed Adieu from Th J. to M.R.

Life's visions are vanished, its dreams are no more;
Dear friends of my bosom, why bathed in tears?
I go to my fathers, I welcome the shore
Which crowns all my hopes or which buries my cares.
Then farewell, my dear, my loved daughter, adieu!
The last pang of liie is in parting from you!
Two seraphs await me long shrouded in death;
I will bear them your love on my last parting breath.[27]

She found her final resting place on the one piece of Monticello she had managed to retain, the burying ground, laid at the head of her father.

Extracts from Martha Jefferson Randolph's Letters After the Death of Her Father

> Since her correspondence with her father is generally available in various editions of his papers, the extracts here focus on her letters to her family after his death, 4 July 1826, mostly from Boston where she would live with her daughter Ellen Coolidge. These extracts are from her correspondence edited by her granddaughter Sarah N. Randolph for the volume, *Worthy Women of Our First Century* (Philadelphia, 1877), 54-60.

1826

[Although written later, this extract describes her emotional state following her father's death:] When my dear father first died, my mind for some time was in the state of one in a vision. I lived over my life with him, every circumstance appeared to pass in review through my memory, and if at that moment my thoughts could have been transmitted to paper, it would have constituted a memoir of his private life more complete and perfect than can ever again be written. The journeys that I had made with him in my childhood were still so fresh in my mind that in traveling the same road afterwards in my journey to Boston I was overwhelmed with melancholy recollections. As much as every object had changed, the old scenes, associated with the names of the places we had visited together, rose fresh in my mind to make the contrast yet more bitter.

Yet I must do myself the justice to say that, great as that contrast was, it was not that, it was not the loss of fortune and of hope but of the being on earth I most idolized, and one of whom the thought had for years past become a habit of my mind. His age and infirmities, and the near termination of that precious life, had long weighed upon my spirits, and the darkness of the future, impervious even to the eye of the imagination, admitted not one ray of light or hope to enlighten the gloom.

November 22. Now that I shall have my mornings free, I can write regularly to you all, dear children of my heart. I have thought of you but once since I left you, and that was from the morning of our sorrowful parting until the present moment. My health, strength, and spirits have all recruited very much. If hope could ever exist again in my heart, I should say that our prospects are brightening. But I shall never expect good fortune until I lay my hand upon it, and even then I shall wash my face to see if I am really awake and not dreaming.

Now that I have become reconciled to the prospect of earning my bread by a school, it remains to be proven whether when the cup of bitterness is actually pressed to my lips I can take it with the same philosophy that I do a necessary medicine that is to restore health. God help me if that fail! I should not long be here to eat the bread of dependence, or to see my children beggars. Upon their success in life I believe mine depends.

Adieu, dearest Virginia. I dare not think of you, or rather give way to my thoughts, anywhere but in the retirement of my own bed chamber; for, though I can command every other demonstration of grief, the tears will occasionally drop from my eyes when I forget to restrain my sad thoughts, which will revert to past, present, and future scenes, all fraught with wretchedness and anxiety. . . . God knows my heart is overflowing with love for many and kindness to all.

December 12. Perhaps I may get one thousand or twelve hundred dollars from Congress, if they see fit to pay a just debt — money actually advanced by my dear father, originally five hundred dollars, now, with interest of twenty years, more than doubled. But that is uncertain, although I have looked to it as a resource to fix up my school.

I have fixed my eye so steadily upon the Gorgon's head that it is producing its effect, and I am every day more callous or more resigned to the drudgery of it. If we should succeed and make anything, those profits might be placed in the funds, so as to give a support for the years in which I may no longer be able to do anything for myself.

Unfortunately, I was educated as the heiress to a great estate and was learning music, etc. etc. when I ought to have been acquiring dexterity with my needle. But I believe no good management of mine could under the circumstances in which we have been placed, have saved the estate, although it might have added, and no doubt would, to the comfort and elegance of our living; but my education may still be the means of procuring us food and raiment.

December 21. I judge from the manner in which George's schoolmaster encourages and praises him that he has never required the spur. I can say with truth that *I* have never eaten one meal in peace since he has been going to school, for his "Come, mamma, we are losing time," rouses me from many a pleasant conversation. Poor little fellow, it is the only trouble he gives me.

December 28. With regard to a removal from the neighborhood, whatever place will be most favorable for our future business will be best for us. Although I still believe we should have the advantage of respect and affection — everything to persons who have lost everything else — in a degree in our own neighborhood, where we are known and appreciated, that as strangers we could hope for nowhere else. But this, after all, is a secondary consideration.

I received a letter from your brother [her own son Jefferson] yesterday of so cheerful a tone that it has made me feel more lighthearted than usual, although he still repeats that we have nothing but our own exertions to depend upon. I have never for one moment believed otherwise; but we are all young [she was 54], and the struggle is over, our minds being made up for the future, and I trust we all have the strength of mind sufficient to make the necessary exertion gracefully and cheerfully.

I hope Jefferson will be able to assist his brothers, at least till *I* can contribute my share. I write that *I* boldly, because with returning health and strength I feel an energy that I trust will not spend itself in words. . . .

Tell my dear Lewis that I have been made truly happy by hearing how steadily he has been going on with his studies since I left; but they have none of them written to me. Ben's energy of character I depend on to make him a useful member of society if properly applied, and I hope James will not be deficient when he sees us all cheerfully laboring for the same end. God bless you, my dear Mary.

Nicholas furnished us with a motto that we ought to adopt: a tree without leaves, and "reflorebo." Brighter days will come. This winter will be very serviceable to us all, and when we meet it will be, I hope, to show ourselves worthy of our origin. Through life I have had a bright example of fortitude, cheerfulness, and dignified resignation to unavoidable evil.

Close of 1826. Comfortable as I am here and sorry as I shall be to leave Ellen, yet, in truth, "Home is home, be it ever so homely," and my heart is constantly hovering around it. For myself, as I must resign the spot which sheltered whilst living and now contains the only earthly remains of my dear, dear father, on my own account I do not care where I go. For your sakes, I wish to do that which is most for your interests, my dear children; but I cannot but look back to Monticello, as Eve did to Paradise after they were driven forth into the wilderness of the world. . . .

Excuse this illegible scrawl, but really, inexplicable as it may seem, I have even less time here than at home, and nothing to show for it. We breakfast at half-past eight; at nine the children are gone, and it is nearly ten before I get to my room; at eleven I dress for morning visitors, we dine at half-past two, and the days are already as short here as they are at their shortest in Virginia.

The broken intervals in the forenoon I mend for the children and myself and write. After dinner I strum a little on the piano and help George and Septimia with their lessons. A most unsatisfactory day it makes and a very idle one. Mr. C[oolidge] insists much on my walking and I really, unless it was the day we played truant from a stupid preacher, have never had time.

1827

January 17. When I return we will determine on our future home — as dear Monticello is out of the question, I presume, for the present at least. I acknowledge I have looked forward to the possibility of returning there at some future day when our income in money, clear of the enormous encumbrance of those large families of negroes, would permit us to control our expenditures; but it has rather been a vague wish than a hope. However, one prospect of more certain happiness is, my dear daughter, that we shall all meet again and be blessed in each other's society. Wherever our home is, there also will be love and harmony. . . .

In writing me the particulars of the sale [of Monticello furniture] tell me what arrangements have been thought of with regard to a residence; for no doubt the subject must have been much talked of and some places suggested as most desirable. Remember, in all deliberations of the kind, that I shall have no choice but the interest of the family. I still think we shall have to keep a school; and wherever we can do the best in that line will be the wisest choice.

January 22. I have been very anxious to hear the particulars of the sale at Monticello and whether the paintings have been taken down yet. My father's two, [son] Jefferson's and mine, will of course remain; Mr. Madison's also — I do not think it would be treating so excellent a friend well to sell it. . . . I should also wish that the gold medal given my father by one of the agricultural societies of France, and the beautiful medal of Bonaparte, and Oliver Cromwell's picture should be retained; also Coffee's bust of Mr. Madison. I hope Jefferson will not think me unreasonable in wishing to retain these. If he thinks it wrong, they must go.

There were some articles of furniture that I should have wished bid in for me, but, except for my dear father's bedroom furniture (not the clock) and what belonged to you girls, and Septimia's and George's little presses that your aunt Jane gave them, I did not think I had a right to keep anything else.

My heart has been continually hovering about that dear home, and my imagination at work with a minuteness of detail that has spared me nothing but the sight. I know it is necessary; I do not repine; but I cannot but remember that such things were and are most dear to me. Do not think that I give way, my dear daughters, to low spirits. You will find that I have as much exertion and self-command as our necessities demand.

I can say no more, nor must you be surprised if at times when I cannot be occupied the unbidden tear will start. The images at the bottom of my heart naturally recur when my attention is not forcibly called from them, and that every hour — nay every moment — of the day.

February 13. The marble clock [over her father's bed] I should have prized beyond anything on earth and if, in our circumstances, I had felt myself justified in retaining a luxury of that value, that clock, in preference to everything else but the immediate furniture of his bedroom, I should have retained. . . .

I am very glad nobody would buy the old sofa, as many a time will my weary limbs rest upon it, without the self-reproach of having retained a luxury, however cheap, that could have been sold. As it was, the high sales of the old furniture showed the kind disposition of the neighborhood to us.

February 19. The approach of spring makes my heart turn to dear home and my still dearer children, only to remember that I have no home and am seven hundred miles from so many objects of my love.

March 21. Oh, how often the words "dear home" tremble upon my lips and dim my eyes! Will it ever again be my home? And until that question is decided, where is our home to be? I believe it would be more convenient for me to remain here till the fall.

Sometime in 1827. In our poverty we have still some of the greatest luxuries of wealth — consideration and respect. I never feel my own dignity more than when in company with a rich *parvenu*. Our poverty is an honorable one. Our wealth, which was great, was not spent in riotous living nor in extravagance, but it was lost by the time and attention which others devote to their private affairs being exclusively devoted by my dear father to his country, in whose service he was worn out. He retired from public life too old to learn and too infirm to attend to his own business; and this, with causes of expense incident to his situation, is sufficient to account for our condition.

1832

Summer. If I had lost the power of walking and eating, for both of which I seem to have renovated powers, I should resemble the unfortunate hen whose brains had been extracted and who sat still and fattened in her stupidity. I have lost my memory entirely but not my taste for reading, and if I forget what I read at least it amuses me for the time, although it leaves but a vague, misty impression.

I have read lately one of the most poetical books of travel I ever met with — Chateaubriand's Itinerary from Paris to Jerusalem. . . . After once having known the happiness of a comfortable home of our own, how bitter is the moment that drives us from it, and how little interest has any other spot after it! A mere resting place for the while, where everything is confined to the present; no future which brings anything but a change of place, nothing to amuse the heart or interest the fancy. If ever I can afford it I will have a permanent residence somewhere, a home, in fine — a feeling I never shall know in a rented house.

Sometime around 1835-36.

My life is a mere shadow as it regards myself. In you [children] alone I live and am attached to it. The useless pleasures which still strew my path with flowers — my love for plants and books — would be utterly heartless and dull but for the happiness which I derive from my affections; these make life still dear to me and will make death painful.

Dolley Madison, from an engraving

DOLLEY PAYNE TODD MADISON

Born Guilford County, North Carolina 20 May 1768, as Dorothea.

Died at Washington, DC, 12 July 1849 of stroke.

Eldest of four daughters among eight children of John and Mary Coles Payne, convert Quaker farmers.

Wed John Todd 7 January 1790, widowed 24 October 1793; wed James Madison 15 September 1794.

One child — John Payne Todd (1792-1852).

DOLLEY PAYNE TODD MADISON

Without Dolley Madison's leadership, Washington society seemed like a magic lantern show, a mere succession of unrelated images. Her dear friend Anna Maria Thornton found it "a most unfavorable place for forming steady attachments, all are newcomers and birds of passage, uninterested in one another and only interested for themselves."[1] Mrs. Madison's great achievement alongside her husband in 40 years of public service was to supply emerging America with a sense of style to unify the nation.

It is not too much to say that almost singlehandedly she endowed the office of president with its peculiar blend of elegance and friendliness. She had been unofficial hostess

for widower Jefferson during his two terms in the White
House and had witnessed the chaos of his policy of maintaining "open house" for all visitors. She had also experienced
the stodgy formality of Martha Washington's receptions,
particularly in the first administration when James Madison
served as Washington's congressional leader.

When her own husband became president, Mrs. Madison
reinstituted Mrs. Washington's practice of weekly receptions, but now graced them with Jefferson's downhome
hospitality. She also introduced her own sense of elegance
— for example, importing silver urns from France for serving
that French delicacy Jefferson had introduced to the White
House dinners, ice cream. More important politically, she
reintroduced Washington's insistence on maintaining political neutrality when the president assumed his ceremonial (as
opposed to political) role.

Madison's friends would of course come to her receptions, but so would his political enemies. The city of
Washington offered little else for them to do during the
winter. White House dinners were doubly appealing to congressmen whose meager salaries kept them cloistered in
boardinghouses.[2] Their alternative entertainment was gambling at the boardinghouse or gambling at the local gambling
halls where a compulsive congressman could lose more than
a year's salary in a single night.

The wives of government officials forced to live in the
federal city, along with those few congressional wives who
could afford to live with their husbands, also gambled. The
newcomer in 1814, Mary Crowninshield, wife of the new navy
secretary, gambled the night away at Mrs. Monroe's; and the
next morning rose with so guilty a conscience that she carried
her good-sized winnings to Mrs. Madison as a donation for
the local orphanage.[3] She soon came to cherish Mrs.
Madison's receptions and dinners.

She described the crush at the New Year's reception in
1815. "It took us ten minutes to push and shove ourselves
through the dining-room; at the upper part of it stood the
President and his lady, all standing — and a continual moving
in and out."[4] Finally reaching the hostess's full attention,

Mrs. Crowninshield had the consummate pleasure of Mrs. Madison's assurance that their tastes in fashion were the same. The First Lady even asked *her* advice on accessories! In that little episode lies the secret of Dolley Madison's success. On visiting the Crowninshield residence and seeing a painting of Mr. Crowninshield, she assured his wife the picture was not so handsome as the original. When author Washington Irving entered a White House reception for the first time, within ten minutes he had made friends with half the persons in the room, impelled by Mrs. Madison's personality.[5]

Irving found the discomfited president looking like "a withered little" winter apple alongside the ebullient hostess and her two lively sisters, bouncing around the guests like two merry wives of Windsor, while the French master-of-ceremonies kept the waiters moving with plenty of food and drinks for those who could not manage to reach the bountiful table.

Another newcomer, Elbridge Gerry, Junior, stood awkwardly about until the hostess, always on the lookout, spotted him. In seconds, she informed him that he was a second cousin — "I felt highly honored," he confided to his diary, "and peculiarly favored."[6] Clearly, she made everybody feel like a kissin' cousin. Noticing another shy youth trying to balance his cup of coffee when the saucer fell on the floor and the cup in his pocket, she hurried over to ask how his mother was, how he liked Washington — while signaling the waiter for another cup of coffee.[7]

That kind of charm turned to political advantage. Rules of good manners cooled the heat of personal and political argument. Her infectious good humor promoted general good feeling. Opposition leaders accepted the fact that she used the reception and dinner to lobby for the president's programs and her own favorite appointments. Still, it was only a question of time before political enemies recognized her as a political opponent.

In the heat of Madison's first campaign, Sam Hunt of New Hampshire hinted that Mrs. Madison's charms skimmed very close to seduction.[8] The President's not very bright ally

Gideon Granger reacted at once by challenging Hunt to a duel for the lady's honor. This blew the hint into a national scandal that never really subsided into silence, and even today surfaces in weird ways. The Georgetown newspaper, *Federal Republican*, was responsible for elaborating the hint into a thinly veiled suggestion that Mrs. Madison's promiscuity was due to her husband's impotency.[9]

We could not know how much the Madison's pillow talk affected the President's policies or practices. Her letters to him show an avid interest in news not only from the capital but from the cabinet, though she assured him, "You know I am not much of a politician" and knew her role.[10] She would not do as some wives did, she said, play the "active partisan." At the same time, she assured her brother that she had to be very careful to avoid political partisanship even in her letters — "I must not trust my pen."[11]

Her circumspection did not escape the keen eye of a visiting teen from New York, Frances Few. As niece of the secretary of the treasury Albert Gallatin she attended a Wednesday night dinner at the White House, duly impressed by "all the great folks of the nation [who] were there" but even more so by the hostess. Mrs. Madison appeared tall, majestic, "a little affected" and "fond of admiration." Yet Frances Few found it was impossible "to be with her and not be pleased."[12]

With a teenager's sensitivity she sensed that Mrs. Madison was playing a role: "I do not think it possible to know what her real opinions are — she is all things to all men, not the least of a prude as she one day told an old bachelor and held up her mouth for him to kiss."

She did, however, manage to develop a network of political wives, as in keeping Albert Gallatin's wife informed of his reconfirmation hearing before the Senate. Yet even Mrs. Madison had her limits. Louis Turreau, French ambassador to this country, had been saved from death during the French Revolution when the jailer's daughter erased the fatal chalk mark signifying that he was to be hung. In return he married her and brought her with him to America. Here, to Mrs. Madison's horror, she learned that "he whips his wife, and abuses her dreadfully."[13] Against diplomatic immunity even Mrs. Madison was powerless.

She did take the lead in civic projects like the Washington orphan asylum which she served for two years as director. Her principal concern was with the ceremonial side of the presidency. From the start, she insisted that her husband's inauguration would be a major social event, even to having the best seats on the floor of Congress reserved for the ladies. They came in all their finery in tribute to the new First Lady who was herself dressed in the latest fashion.

She began the tradition of the modern inaugural ball, taking over Long's Hotel on Capitol Hill for the event. Before 400 guests at precisely seven o'clock in the evening, Mrs. Madison made a grand entrance, enchanting the crowd in her gown of buff velvet and white satin "with two superb plumes [of] the bird of paradise feathers."[14] She looked like a queen.

There was hardly room to breathe, much less dance, and the crowd broke out the windows for air. Mrs. Madison confessed that she had never learned to dance, and her husband was overheard confiding, "I would much rather be in bed."[15]

Being First Lady meant much more than throwing parties. As pace setter, she gave up her favorite simple caps such as her Quaker forbears wore. As "presidentess", she adopted the latest French turbans. More important, friends began noticing other changes in her day- to-day living: "She visits less," said one, "and indulges less in her favorite amusement of cards."[16] The success of her non-partisan policy meant that in the White House, according to Jonathan Roberts of Pennsylvania, "you cannot discover who is her husband's friends or foes."[17] She played the role of presidentess of the entire nation.

The whole nation in return took her to our collective bosom, especially after her heroism in the British attack on the nation's capital, Summer 1814. "Tho' a Quaker," said she, "I have always been an advocate for fighting when assailed."[18] She stood her ground in the White House until the enemy's direct approach, then she decamped. Her husband was away viewing the action elsewhere, so she gathered up the silver and files of secret papers plus a portrait of George Washington. She and the nation believed it to be an original by Gilbert Stuart of his famous _Lansdowne_ portrait. It was only a copy by William Winstanly,[19] but she knew its value as an icon to the nation.

She fled to join her husband and for a couple of days they pursued each other through the forests of Virginia. He had retreated to a tavern near McLean where they were supposed to rendezvous, except she stopped on the way to visit her friend Matilda Love, then took a wrong turn, leaving Madison in panic when she failed to turn up at the tavern. He hurried to Falls Church hoping she was there, then returned to the tavern, catching up with her at last.

They returned to find the capital a mess, the White House demolished — "unroofed naked walls, cracked, defaced and blackened with fire."[20] Yet the only icon the enemy took away was a miniature painting of Dolley Madison herself. For the next two- and-a-half years of her husband's presidency, they would stay in the sumptuous Octagon House on what would today be called Society Row.

There, as soon as she could, Mrs. Madison renewed her weekly receptions as a boost to wartime morale. With news of the first American victories, she invited the whole nation to an open house. As Madison's second term came to a close, the people of Georgetown gave her a separate public ball.

Their estate at Montpelier, though only 93 miles away, provided an idyllic setting for retirement where they could surround themselves with great books and a world-class collection of fine art acquired during 43 years of diplomacy and public service. Aloof here from party politics they were, none the less, overrun with visitors: "I am," she said, "less worried here with a hundred visitors than with twenty-five in Washington."[21]

Surrounded by books, Madison was in his element. He carried on a lively correspondence and did attend the Virginia constitutional convention of 1829, making his usual appeal for national unity and as usual being ignored. Although in declining health, in 1834 he dictated to Dolley his masterful statement, "Advice to My Country," a practice of dictating to her that he had followed even when President. Now she took on the added burden of nursing him for the next two years. With Madisonian diffidence, he died one morning at breakfast, "as quietly as the snuff of a candle goes out," 28 June 1836.[22] Dolley Madison was a widow again.

She would live another thirteen years. Two years of nursing a dying husband had sapped her ebullience, and an eye infection made her wear a patch on one eye, but it was only a matter of months before she returned to the social whirl still wearing the turbans she had popularized, now long after they were fashionable. She kept up appearances to the end despite financial ruin that must have created a sense of déja vu, for that had been her condition when her first husband died 43 years earlier.

After two years of a romantic marriage to struggling Philadelphia lawyer, John Todd, she had watched him wither away from yellow fever in October 1793. Dying within a month of his mother and father, two weeks before the stillbirth of his own second son, he left her destitute with a twenty-month-old John Payne Todd, Junior, thereafter just plain "Payne." She had to pay costs for the stillbirth and had only nineteen dollars to her name, not even enough to rejoin her own mother.

Her husband's brother grabbed whatever property the young couple had managed to acquire, even contested the will that explicitly left everything to "the dear wife of my bosom and first and only woman upon whom all my affections were placed." The romantic husband had been certain she would prove "an affectionate mother to my little Payne" and "educate him in the ways of honesty . . . better to him than a name and riches."[23]

Despite the will, James Todd managed to tie up her estate, slight as it was, for two years — and only then came to agreement when her new husband, Madison, put pressure on him. Both property and money were put in Payne's name, and James Todd would leave her ever after. Marrying wealthy bachelor Madison of course meant that she would be well-off, for he had his own five thousand acre plantation. A decade earlier he had overcome his scholarly shyness to propose to a sixteen-year-old Kitty Floyd, who had turned him down for a young medical student. That summer of 1794, however, Dolley Payne Todd had charmed him once more out of his scholarly shell for both their sakes.

She confided to her friend Eliza Collins that the man she teased (about his height) as "her great little Madison" was "the man who of all others I most admire."[24] She knew he would prove "a generous and tender protector" to little Payne. How generous a protector became clear after Madison's will was read. His widow knew that he had paid $20,000 to clear the young man's gambling debts. Now she learned that he had paid another $20,000 in secret to avoid giving her further grief over Payne's dissolute life. She herself had also been taking secret loans to bail him out of debt for at least a quarter-century.

An apologist for Payne might point out that he grew up spoiled by a mother who had already lost a beloved husband and infant son and whose home, wherever, was a continuous round of wining, dining, fun and games. In his thirties Payne did try to cure himself of addiction to alcohol and gambling but without success. Now with his widowed mother completely at his mercy the end was inevitable. Even the papers that Madison had laboriously prepared for sale to Congress after his death were milked for piecemeal profits. Payne was relentless.

He sold off bits and pieces of Montpelier, first secretly, then openly, with its paintings and objects of art going for a pittance. The only time Mrs. Madison objected was when he tried to sell the family silver. Otherwise she seemed willing to indulge him to the brink of bankruptcy — her own. His grandest design was construction of an ornate estate for both of them with special provision for entertaining in her old style. This project, too, ran out of money.

Even so, Mrs. Madison continued to entertain in her little house in Washington, explaining to one visitor that she had "few possessions in life except poor kin."[25] In the 1840s she was one of the capital's wonders. Congress voted her the privilege of sitting on the House floor anytime. Nor was she merely a relic of bygone days. She continued to play an influential role as social arbiter. She also became guide, tutor and confidante to a succession of First Ladies. Her niece, Elizabeth Singleton, President Van Buren's daughter-in-law, depended on her. So did President Tyler's daughter-in-law after his wife died and the young lady was thrust into the role of nation's hostess.[26] Dolley Madison had become an institution for just such occasions, a First Lady for forty years.

When Jessie Benton Frémont, still another cousin, remembered Mrs. Madison in her "shabby old gowns of velvet or brocade nowise altered from the fashion of her days of power,"[27] it was not to ridicule — nor were mentions of her rouge and powder or false black curls that were meant to camouflage old age. In spite of these cartoonlike features, Mrs. Madison impressed even critical schoolgirls with her charm.

"While she was talking with the more distinguished people her quick eye would mark some shy young man or nervous-looking woman, not yet used to society . . . in her own bright way [she] said something . . . which made them glow with the pleased feeling that they were welcome," that they were the most important persons there.[28]

She never lost her sense of play. A young nephew recalled a family tradition. He believed she never grew older because every year when he went to her birthday party, he would ask her age and every year would be told the same answer. She also told him that the statue of Jefferson in the hall went to dinner whenever it heard the bell ring. The boy would sit for hours watching that statue before ultimately realizing that the statue "never hears the bell ring."[29]

Her final public appearance, appropriately enough, was at President Polk's reception just before he retired. She entered the stage for this last scene sweeping in elegantly on the President's arm while the crowd bowed in homage. She outlived even Polk by a month, dying peacefully of a stroke in early July 1849, age eighty-one, not the last of the Founding Mothers but kissin' cousin of us all.

Extracts from Dolley Madison's Letters

1811 Washington

November 15. [To Ruth and Joel Barlow in Paris where Barlow was sent to negotiate a treaty of commerce with Napoleon:] Your short notes which gave us an account of your progress on the water were grateful indeed, but the news of your safe arrival in France infinitely more so. Many, many are the questions that rise to my lips — such as, how did you bear the voyage? how is our precious Clara [Barlow], Mr. Barlow, Mr. Lee? I hope soon to know these things, which I confess interests *me* more than all the success of your mission of which few have a doubt. Even the enemies of *our* Minister [i.e., Barlow] admit his talents and virtue. How then can any of *them* doubt?

We passed two months on our mountain in health and peace, returned the first of October to a sick and afflicted city. The unfinished canal caused a bilious fever to prevail almost through all its streets. Many died and Congress convened in some dread of contagion. Happily all fears are now over and public business engrosses them. John R[andolph] is the only one (as yet) who seems hostile to a quick House. They have before them the nomination of Colonel M — — —- and some lesser appointments. I believe they are in disposition to do as they are advised.

The judges are not yet made. Mr. Duball is thought of for Maryland and, Mr. Adams having declined to return or accept, gives an opportunity for G — — — — —- to try again. I am sorry to tell you of the translation of the Pahlens to Rio Janeiro. Mr. Dashcoff takes their place [as Russian envoy].

The French Minister is still delighted with Kalirama and takes pleasure in beautifying the grounds. Mrs. Baldwin, who came to see me and whom I visited, was well and cheerful a few days ago. She will write you a volume no doubt, and she will tell you of the health of your little dog. Many others will write you, my dear friend, and leave me but little to inform you of. Mr. M[adison] is writing also — he will tell you that he has settled the business of the Chesapeake with Mr. Foster etc. etc.

Tell our estimable Lee that — — — —- conduct has not injured him here. On the contrary, it excited a horror of the "persecutor" and we trust that Heaven will prosper him and his family.

I have not yet begun my Journal as I had nothing remarkable to narrate. Mr. Barlow knows the disposition of *our world* better than I do, and from all I learn good sense and principle will prevail over *intrigue* and *vanity*. The instance of Mr. R.S. is striking. The poor man is down! Madame Bon[aparte], too, who has been some weeks in town, says *she is on our side.*

You will see that Colvin declares himself the author of the boasted letters. Some think this a finishing stroke, but I absolutely pity him, for he has "fallen, fallen from his high estate"!

We have new members in abundance — their wives, daughters, etc. etc. and I never felt the entertainment of company oppressive until now. Oh! I with I was in France with you, for a little relaxation. My sister [Lucy] Washington is with me but never will forgive me refusing to let her go with you. But I know it is better for her to remain with me. My poor brother has been ill ever since you left us, until now.

As you have everything that is beautiful — and we have nothing — I will ask the favor of you to send me by safe vessels: large head-dresses, a few flowers, feathers, gloves, and stockings (black and white), or any other pretty things suitable to an economist — and draw on my husband [i.e. his account] for the amount. . . . [BN 343]

1812 Washington

April 20. [To Ruth and Joel Barlow in Paris:] Before this, you know of our embargo, to be followed by War! Yes, that terrible event ["will take place" is crossed out] is at hand, and yet England wants faith! Our appointments for the purpose are generally made [lists general officers] . . . .

You will have an account of our political situation in all its shades by the vessel [the ship *Constitution*]. We anticipate some little contention among ourselves on the death of the Vice President, whose physicians give out that he cannot live till morning! The sentiment is, at present, in favor of John Langdon as his successor.

Congress will remain in session perhaps till July. If not, full powers to declare war will be vested in the President.

Your letters by the *Neptune* were particularly acceptable as we had been annoyed by a report that the Emperor had seized the *Hornet* etc. etc. And as I *promised* to write you things you ought to know, you will pardon me when I say what gives you pain. I am preparing you for the disapprobation expressed at Mr. Barlow's having *told* the state of his negotiations to Mr. Granger who directly gave it circulation and a place in the newspapers. In the *detail* of objections to *this* communication is "that you may yet be disappointed," "that Mr. G. was not a proper channel," etc. etc. All this is from the *people* not from the Cabinet, yet you know everything *vibrates* there.

Tell Mr. Lee that I shall be ever grateful for the fatigue and trouble he must have experienced for my sake in procuring the valuable collection he sent me. His bill was paid immediately, but he will be astonished at the whole amount — duties, etc. etc., two thousand dollars. I am afraid that I shall never send for anything more.

The dresses and every other article, indeed, is beautiful. The head[dress]es I could not get on, being too tight around. Their price was so high that the ladies of my acquaintance would neither buy or swap one, so that I shall lay them by for next winter, and then enlarge to make them fit. My shoes were just a size too short, but the flowers, trimmings and ornaments were enchanting.

I wish I could gratify you, my dear friend, with the portraits you mention, but I see little prospect of doing so. Stuart is far from us and we have no painter of skill in this quarter. Be assured, if an opportunity occurs, I will employ it to send you such as you shall approve.

You have kindly recollected my dear [sister] Lucy. She was married on the 30th of March to Judge Todd and left me on the next day for Lexington in Kentucky. I have been filled with *selfish* regrets. Her union is a most happy one and met our entire approbation. Her husband is of the Supreme

Court and obliged to pass a great deal of time here, which lessens *my* misfortune. He is amiable, intelligent, in short, he is all that I could wish in a brother. John has gone with them, and you now see *me*, the *very* shadow of my husband.

My sister [Anna] Cutts did not visit us the last winter, but she will soon be here to console me; so that, as ever, my prospect is tinctured with hope. . . . [BN 344]

1814 Washington

August 23. [describing for sister Lucy Washington Todd what happened when the British attacked the White House:] My husband left me yesterday morning to join General Winder. He enquired anxiously whether I had courage, or firmness, to remain in the President's House until his return on the morrow or succeeding day, and on my assurance that I had no fear but for him and the success of our army, he left me, beseeching me to take care of myself and of the cabinet papers, public and private. I have since received two despatches from him written with a pencil. The last is alarming, because he desires I should be ready at a moment's warning to enter my carriage and leave the city; that the enemy seemed stronger than had been reported, and that it might happen they would reach the city with intention to destroy it. . . .

I am accordingly ready. I have pressed as many cabinet papers into trunks as to fill one carriage. Our private property must be sacrificed, as it is impossible to procure wagons for its transportation. I am determined not to go myself until I see Mr. Madison safe, and he can accompany me — as I hear of much hostility towards him . . . disaffection stalks around us.

My friends and acquaintances are all gone, even Colonel C— — —, with his hundred men who were stationed as a guard in this enclosure. . . . French John [Sioussat], with his usual activity and resolution, offers to spike the cannon at the gate and to lay a train of powder which would blow up the British should they enter the house. To the last proposition I positively object, without being able, however, to make him understand why all advantages in war may not be taken.

Wednesday morning twelve oclock. Since sunrise I have been turning my spy glass in every direction and watching with unwearied anxiety, hoping to discern the approach of my dear husband and his friends, but alas I can descry only groups of military wandering in all directions, as if there was a lack of arms or of spirit to fight for their own firesides!

Three oclock. Will you believe it my sister? We have had a battle, or skirmish, near Bladensburg, and I am still here within sound of the cannon! Mr. Madison comes not — may God protect him! Two messengers, covered with dust, come to bid me fly, but I wait for him. . . .

At this late hour, a wagon has been procured. I have had it filled with the plate and most valuable portable articles belonging to the house. Whether it will reach its destination, and Bank of Maryland, or fall into the hands of the British soldiery, events must determine.

Our kind friend, Mr. Carroll, has come to hasten my departure and is in a very bad humor with me because I insist on waiting until the large picture of General Washington is secured, and it requires to be unscrewed from the wall. This process was found too tedious for these perilous moments. I have ordered the frame to be broken and the canvas taken out. It is done — and the precious portrait placed in the hands of two gentlemen of New York for safe keeping. And now, dear sister, I must leave this house, or the retreating army will make me a prisoner in it by filling up the road I am directed to take. When I shall again write to you, or where I shall be tomorrow, I cannot tell. National Portrait Gallery (Philadelphia, 1836) 3:7-8]

1824, Montpelier, Virginia

December 2. [to her son John Payne Todd:] Mr. Clay with two members of Congress left us yesterday after passing two days — Mr. C inquired affectionately after you, as does all your acquaintance whom I see. But, my dear son, it seems to be the wonder of them all that you should stay so long from us. And now I am ashamed to tell you when asked how long my only child has been absent from the home of his mother!

Your Papa and myself entreat you to come to us; to

arrange your business with those concerned to return to them when necessary, and let us see you here as soon as possible with your interest — [and] convenience. Your Papa thinks as I do that it would be best for your reputation and happiness as well as ours that you should have the appearance of consulting your parents on subjects of deep account to you, and that you should find it so in *returning* to Philadelphia when you appointed, to choose to do so. I have said in my late letters as well as this all that *I thought sufficient* to influence you. I must now put my trust in God alone!

If the young lady you have followed so long has not yet been won, I fear she wants the character, son, to favor your happiness hereafter, though others might be found who would.

I enclose $30 instead of 20 which you mentioned, and though I am sure 'tis insufficient for the journey, I am unable to add to the sum today. I recently paid Holloway $200 on your note, with interest for two years. The other small debts in the quarter I settled long ago with funds of yours in my hands.

I hope you will write me the moment you get this that I may know certainly your determinations and make up my own. I can add no news that is likely to interest you except that poor Judge Todd is likely to die and that Ellen Randolph is to be married to Mr. Coolidge. "The bright ocurrence" you allude to I hope is propitious (if it were for your good we might rejoice in your immediate union provided it brought you speedily to our arms who love with inexpressible tenderness and constancy). [Facsimile in H.T. Upton, *Our Early Presidents, Their Wives and Children* (Boston, 1890) 233]

1844 Washington

May 22. [To her son, like the two following extracts, derived from A.C. Clark, *Life and Letters of Dolly Madison (Washington, 1914):*] [George] Dromgole and John Y. Mason came to see me yesterday about the papers, saying that many were anxious to vote me the amount with which I would be satisfied could I name it. I was at a loss from delicacy and a want of knowledge to name.

They mentioned the sum for [her late husband's notes on the Federal Constitution] Debates but I did not reply farther, hoping to obtain an answer from you to my late letters in which I wished you to advise. They wanted the letter explaining the reasons for the veto on the Bank after adhering long to a contrary opinion. Will you now tell me if I should let the Committee see that explanatory letter and what other letters I had best show them as specimens of the writings and the sum expected for them — stereotype and all — what to say of copyright? They and others advise that the sale of these papers should be consummated "in my time" and during this session [of Congress]. I have given no direct answer but told them I wanted you here to act for me and to enlighten me as to one more point, whether they could have the letters or some of them to Mr. M....

Oh, that you, my beloved, were fixed in all things to cooperate with me. I will not say to act solely for me, because I had become the object of interest and less would be done without me. This is one of the opportunities so seldom allowed, wherein it is proper for persons to speak *well* of themselves, and I therefore have and will repeat to you these facts as necessary to be taken into view. I want your reply a few days — five. Your last said nothing in answer to my six last.... [338-39]

1848 Washington

May 21. You have seen by the gazettes, my dear son, that we had an alarm of fire in our house on last Saturday week. At 4 oclock in the morning our chamber door was assailed by [servant] Ralph who begged [niece] Annie and myself to come down immediately whilst the stairs remained. We did so through a crackling fire. Losing not a moment, we reached the garden ground.

He returned and brought me down the trunk of papers, when our neighbors (just awakened) came to our assistance and soon separated the fire from the window frame in which it had made great progress. It has been supposed to be the work of an incendiary, and the watch is nightly round the city.

Yesterday Congress passed the bill for the purchase of

Mr. Madison's papers — I will enclose you the newspapers.
. . . [419-20]

July 10. [To her son:] I ardently hoped that you would
have written me about our affairs before this, and that I
should have some guide to lead from whelming darkness —
but it is in vain to wait! I wish to tell you all that concerns us,
but you are silent about your being at home or absent from
it.

I have concluded to have a raffle for the large painting
with other pictures and some plate in order to be better
satisfied, etc. What ought the large painting and those of
Washington and Jefferson by Stuart to bring in a raffle or
sale? Those of Adams and Monroe also? Please give some
guess and tell what estimate you place upon Columbus,
Vespucius, Magellan, Cortez, and the Bard of Ossian.

I wrote you a week ago but no answer has come to me,
though 'twas important I should have one. [433]

Autobiographical Note

[For a biographical piece in the *National Portrait Gallery*
published by Herrick & Longacre in Philadelphia (1836),
Mrs. Madison submitted this sketch to her friend Margaret
Bayard Smith. It is from Mrs. Smith's letters, edited by
Gaillard Hunt (London, 1906) as *Forty Years of Washington
Society*, 351- 52:]

My family are all Virginians except myself, who was born
in North Carolina, whilst my parents were there on a visit of
one year to an uncle. Their families on both sides were
among the most respectable and they, becoming members of
the Society of Friends [Quakers] soon after their marriage
manumitted their slaves, and left this state for Pennsylvania,
bearing with them their children to be educated in their
religion.

I believe my age at that time was 11 or 12 years. I was
educated in Philadelphia, where I was married to Mr. Todd
in 1790 and to Mr. Madison in '94 — when I returned with
him to the soil of my Father and to Washington, where you
have already traced me with the kindness of a sister.

In the year '91, and after the death of my father, my

mother received into her house some gentlemen as boarders, and in '93 she left Philadelphia to reside with her daughter Washington — afterwards with my sister Jackson, and occasionally with me. I am sensible that this is but a general answer to yours. Should any particular information be desired, I will endeavor to furnish it. . . . [Montpelier 31 August 1834]

Elizabeth Hamilton, from the painting by Inman

ELIZABETH SCHUYLER HAMILTON

Born 7 August 1757 at Albany, New York.

Died Washington, D.C. 9 November 1854, buried New York City.

Second daughter of eleven children, with three dying in infancy, born to General Philip Schuyler and Catherine Van Rensselaer Schuyler.

Wed Alexander Hamilton 14 December 1780.

Eight children — Philip (1782-1801), Angelica (1784-1857), Alexander (1786-1875), James (1788-1878), John (1792-1882), William (1797-1850), Eliza (1799-1859), Philip (1802-1884).

ELIZABETH SCHUYLER HAMILTON

During the summer of 1837 in her eightieth year, Elizabeth Schuyler Hamilton visited her son William on the Wisconsin frontier at a camp called Hamilton's Diggings. To get there meant voyaging by stage coach from New York to Pittsburgh then by steamer down the Ohio to Cincinnati and up the Mississippi to Galena (now in Illinois).

With her daughter, Eliza Holley, and son-in-law, she visited till mid- September, seeing as much of the wild frontier as she could because, she said, "She might not have a long time to see things of this world in."[1] Yet she would go on another dozen years, energetic as ever.

The troops at Fort Snelling found the octogenarian especially delightful. They took her on a superb tour of the region — Lake Calhoun, Minnehaha Falls — and she never tired.[2] On the parade ground, they set up an easy chair for her, but she preferred to review the troops by passing between their double columns to the strains of the military band. She took it all as tribute to the memory of their beloved late General Alexander Hamilton. She would not let him be forgotten for the world.

His death by dueling in 1804 had left her with considerable debts, six little children, and three months pregnant. His old allies helped with the debts, but by her own efforts she raised their five boys and two girls as a prudent, industrious single parent insisting on her independence and the sanctity of his good name.

Prudent management of her meager means enabled her to sell off the property her parents had left her little by little until she had put three of the boys through Columbia into successful law careers. When that source of funds dried up, those sons were able to support her and to train their youngest brother to be another lawyer.

The son William she visited in Wisconsin was the non-lawyer. He had dropped out after two years at West Point, lighting out for the Territory as surveyor of government lands, moving with the frontier.[3] He served in the early Illinois legislature and led a troop of Menominee Indian scouts in the Black Hawk War before moving on to serve in the Wisconsin legislature while speculating in mining and smelting lead.

The daughter Eliza with her on the visit was the younger of the two girls. The elder, Angelica, had gone out of her mind after hearing that her brother Philip died dueling. That happened in 1801, three years before Alexander Hamilton died in the same way — and even in the same place, Weehawken, New Jersey. Angelica spent the rest of her life conversing with her dead brother, being cared for at home until late in life when immured in a Long Island asylum.[4] She died at

73, only a few years after her mother.

Mrs. Hamilton's own mother, born Catherine "Kitty" Van Rensselaer, had been the belle of the Hudson Valley in upstate New York. Her marriage to Philip Schuyler had united wealthy and powerful families on both sides of the river. The Schuylers had 11 children, Elizabeth (called Betsy before her marriage) being the second of five girls, all inheriting their mother's strong-willed personality.

Kitty Schuyler became legendary in the Valley for her daring defiance of British troops swooping down on the Schuylers' summer home near Saratoga.[5] On roads clogged with refugees fleeing Burgoyne's army heading southward, she drove her little carriage northward with only one armed guard. She somehow managed to save family treasures and also set fire to the fields to keep the British from harvesting the grain.

When a gang of Loyalists attacked the Schuylers' Albany mansion, the family retreated upstairs to barricaded safety, only to find they had forgotten to bring three-month-old Catherine. Sister Peggy dashed back downstairs, disdaining the raiders, retrieving baby Catherine, and dodging a tomahawk that narrowly missed her own head, leaving a mark on the mahogany bannister that also became legendary in the Valley.

Unlike her lively sisters, Betsy was "quiet, unobtrusive, kindly"[6] in manner, with the delicate features, deep dark eyes, and low soft voice of her beautiful mother, but without her beauty. Visitors remarked on her natural simplicity and gentleness, "the finest tempered girl in the World."[7]

Of the Schuyler girls, she was the homebody, pretty much relieving her mother of household management. She did, however, go with her sisters to visit their friend Kitty Livingston at Elizabeth Town, New Jersey, not far from General Washington's headquarters at Morristown. Their uncle was Washington's surgeon-general, so it was only natural that the girls would visit the camp often and that they would attract the young officers on Washington's staff.

Elizabeth attracted Hamilton. A few months before meeting her, he had joked: "Do I want a wife? No, I have

plagues enough without desiring to add that *greatest of all*."[8]
A few months after meeting her, he had to confess, "I am a
lover in earnest."[9] Though not a genius, he said, Betsy had
"good sense enough to be agreeable," and though not a
beauty, had what it takes to make a lover happy.

They were wed in the Dutch Reformed Church at Albany,
December 1780, in wartime. The formal wedding was unusual in a family where the girls usually eloped, but that does
not mean Betsy was less sentimental. At her death 75 years
later, they found her wearing a tiny bag around her neck
carrying a poem Hamilton had written before their wedding
on paper later grown so fragile she had stitched the pieces
together with thread:

ANSWER TO THE INQUIRY WHY I SIGHED
Before no mortal ever knew
A love like mine so tender- true-
Completely wretched- you away-
And but half blessed e'en while you stay.

If present love . . . face
Deny you to my fond embrace
No joy unmixed my bosom warms
But when my angel's in my arms.[10]

After a month's marriage, she reported to her sisters: "My
dear Hamilton is fonder of me every day — get married!"[11]

Very few of her love letters to him survive, but his letters
to her speak of a marriage solid in love and mutual respect.
Whatever cynics may have said about his motives in marrying
this plain, twenty-three-year old heiress — social, political,
financial connections — he recognized her invaluable assets
in managing the family, minding the store while he was off
winning the war, constructing constitutions, and financing the
Western world. His pal James McHenry told him, "She has
as much merit as your treasurer as you have as treasurer of
the wealth of the United States."[12]

The major strain in their marriage must have come in
1797 when he published a pamphlet confessing that a few

years earlier he had committed adultery with a shady person named Maria Reynolds.[13] Hamilton claimed that she seduced him so that her husband could blackmail him. His enemies claimed Hamilton concocted that alibi to cover the fact of giving Reynolds information for inside trading to their mutual profit.[14]

In the pamphlet Hamilton acknowledged his shame for the pain he inflicted on "a bosom eminently entitled to all my gratitude, fidelity, and love." He assured the public she would forgive this exposure of his sins. Indeed a relative did report to him that the exposé made "not the least Impression on her, only that she considers the whole Knot opposed to you to be Scoundrels."[15]

Washington gossip, however, reported that she was offering to pay second-hand book dealers up to five dollars for every copy of Hamilton's pamphlet so that she could destroy them all. One year, she discovered some unscrupulous dealer in New York had been doing a lively trade in reprinting copies of the pamphlet for ten cents each and selling them to her for five dollars.[16]

For her to have afforded that sort of enterprise seems in character. Hamilton had left real estate worth about $80,000 along with debts of $55,000. His allies took over the debts, and her sisters and brothers signed over shares of their parents' estates. After much petitioning, Congress voted her $10,000 in General Hamilton's back pay plus interest, so she was hardly destitute.[17] Her prudent management kept the family intact in the manner to which they had become accustomed while he had lived.

She even became one of New York's celebrated philanthropists for her pioneering work in behalf of the city's widows and especially orphans. A founding director of the Orphan Asylum Society in 1806, she later succeeded Joanna Bethune as executive director of the Society, serving for 28 years more after a quarter-century's service as Mrs. Bethune's vice-president. Both very strong willed women, she and Mrs. Bethune would argue heatedly over policy and procedures until Mrs. Hamilton, the more impulsive, would embrace her antagonist, concluding the argument with love and kisses and reinvigorated confidence.[18]

In respect to Hamilton's fame, however, she would never give in. To her, his name took on the aura of sanctification. Then, too, unquenchable fame would enhance the value of his papers when, as with Madison's papers, they were offered for sale and publication. That is why she turned for advice to George Washington's nephew, Bushrod, asking how he had managed the sale of the General's papers and seeking the name of a proper literary person to edit the papers and prepare a biography.[19]

As happened, she ran through a stable of literary persons, among them the famous composer Joseph Hopkinson, New York *Post* editor William Coleman, political scientist Timothy Pickering, and even her clergyman Francis Baylies. None could finish the task. She thereupon turned to her sons. Led by John Church Hamilton, they scoured the nation for Hamilton's correspondence and published two volumes by 1840.

When compiling the papers, one of the executors had uncovered drafts of Washington's Farewell Address in Hamilton's handwriting. At once, he sent them to politically powerful Rufus King for safekeeping, for rumors had been circulating that Mrs. Hamilton believed the Address had indeed been composed by her beloved husband.[20]

In the court battle to regain the papers from the King family after Rufus King's death, her heated insistence on Hamilton's authorship antagonized even such old friends as John Jay who had worked with Hamilton on drafting the Address. He testified before a scholarly committee evaluating her claim in 1826. He said Hamilton worked from Washington's earlier draft, adding and correcting, then discussing it with Jay until both were satisfied before submitting it to the president.[21]

Many years later she composed her own version of the event: "He was in the habit of calling me to sit with him, that he might read to me as he wrote." He wanted to hear how it sounded, telling her, "You must be to me what Moliére's old nurse was to him"[22] — an allusion to Moliére's practice of reading to his old housekeeper, gauging by her reaction whether the play would be a hit on stage.

She went on: " The whole or nearly all of the Address was read to me by him as he wrote it and a greater part if not all was written by him in my presence." Surviving manuscripts show that Washington retained about 65 per cent of the draft Hamilton submitted to him. If the thoughts were Washington's, the words were Hamilton's, just as the first inaugural address in 1789 was in the words of Madison — who also wrote the address by Congress to the president and the president's reply to that address![23]

The critics' chief concern was that Mrs. Hamilton's crusade might demean the celebrated Farewell Address, but wiser heads among her antagonists decided to maintain a studied silence. Her tenacity could terrify, as James Monroe found when he came calling to apologize for his part in persecuting Hamilton over the Maria Reynolds scandal.

Called from her garden, she said loud enough for him to hear, "What has that man come to see me for?" She let him into the parlor but would not offer him a chair. He said he hoped time had healed his offense. She heatedly replied: "Mr. Monroe . . . no lapse of time, no nearness to the grave, makes any difference." He left noiselessly.[24]

This careful tending of Hamilton's fame was more than mere memorializing. It was clearly part of trying to sustain her sons and daughters independently, a commitment that dominated her life for a half-century, only occasionally letting her own light peep from behind his luminous shadow.

In 1849, she left New York to join her now widowed daughter Eliza Holley in Washington where they lived next door to heroic General Winfield Scott, who made a great point of calling formally — as most of Washington did — on New Years Day upon both Mrs. Hamilton and Dolley Madison.[25] Unlike Dolley Madison, Elizabeth Hamilton returned few visits and seldom socialized.

President Polk's diary reports her coming to an informal dinner at the White House when she was 88, astonishing him as a "very remarkable person" with perfect intellect and memory for one so old.[26] He added, "My conversation with her was highly interesting." And she could likewise entertain the neighborhood children.[27] Teaching one little girl to play backgammon, she mentioned she had been taught to play by Benjamin Franklin — who visited her father while on the way to persuade Canadians to join the Revolution.

She also recalled how, as a 15-year-old, she had been adopted by neighboring Indians on the New York frontier and given the name "Conadeso," meaning "One of us," and, yes, it was true that unfriendly Indians had massacred settlers on that frontier. She willingly suffered journalists' interviews also, answering questions about such celebrities of the Revolution as Molly Pitcher.[28]

Even more valuable were her recollections of Martha Washington who was, she confessed, "always my ideal of a true woman."[29] She remembered how kind Mrs. Washington had been to her as a young war bride but especially how she and the First Lady had shared "a passionate love of home and domestic life" while trying to play the game of official hostess. She recollected Mrs. Washington's words, "They call me the First Lady in the Land . . . . They might more properly call me Chief State Prisoner."[30]

The journalist-historian Benson J. Lossing called her "The last living belle of the Revolution,"[31] but he saw only the social veneer. More revealing were her repeated attempts to retrieve son William's body from California. He had left Wisconsin to go with the Forty Niners. Settling in Weaver Basin, he opened a trading post, and in one year cleared an estimated $20,000 in gold. One day he left camp for a business trip to Sacramento. Nobody heard from him again. He turned up dead of dysentery unknown in a tiny room of a Sacramento hotel called Our House.[32]

In that plague season of 1850 his body was tossed into a common trench along with fifty other dysentery and cholera corpses. His mother insisted he be exhumed and shipped home at any cost, but could find no shipmaster who would transport the body. In 1889 it was finally given proper ceremonial burial in tribute to William's own memory in Hamilton Square, Sacramento where the brass plaque remains — ironically bearing the likeness of Alexander Hamilton, as though in unintended tribute to the dedication and determined effort of Elizabeth Hamilton to make us remember him.

Before her own death and subsequent burial beside him in Trinity churchyard, Washington's Church of the Epiphany devoted one Sunday service to commemorating her work with orphans. Too feeble to sit through the whole service, she entered for communion — "a very small, upright little figure in deep black" — on the arm of her daughter. The entire congregation rose as one in homage, at last, to Elizabeth Hamilton in her own rite.[33]

Extracts from Elizabeth Hamilton's Letters And Her Interview with Benjamin Lossing

1789 New York

November 8. [To her sister Angelica embarking for England with husband John B. Church, this rare survival of her early letters was a postscript to Alexander Hamilton's letter:]

My very dear beloved Angelica — I have seated myself to write to you, but my heart is so saddened by your absence that it can scarcely dictate, my eyes so filled with tears that I shall not be able to write you much, but *Remember Remember*, my dear sister, of the assurances of your returning to us, and do all you can to make your absence short. Tell Mr. Church for me of the happiness he will give me in bringing you to me, not to me alone but to fond parents, sisters, friends, and to my Hamilton who has for you all the affection of a fond own brother. [*Papers of Alexander Hamilton*, ed. H.C. Syrett (New York, 1961-87), 20:502]

1827 New York

May 11. [To son James A. Hamilton who printed it in his *Reminiscences* (New York, 1869), 64:] As I think my wants will not require your enclosed check until the autumn, let me say to you that when I shall require your goodness to aid me I will call upon you. As all good acts are recorded in the habitation where your father now is, I have no doubt this one will be proclaimed to him, and have thus given him another motive to implore continued blessings upon you. Amen, my dear son! Your affectionate mother.

1836 New York

October 24. [To the same son, in his *Reminiscences*, 289:] How devotedly have I in my mind's eye followed the movements of the ship that contained the favorite son of my beloved departed husband. How often must your mind have been raised to that Great Disposer of the universe who was guarding you on your perilous voyage. Could my wishes have wafted you more swiftly and smoothly than a bird, your passage would soon have terminated. I have greatly feared your delicate lungs would suffer from sea- sickness. . . .

I hope you will have time to examine the police of London. Something may be observed beneficial to this city. My grand- daughters frequently visit me; they are both in good health. . . .

1840 New York

August 7. [Her statement about her husband's writing Washington's "Farewell Address":] Desirous that my children should be fully acquainted with the services rendered by their father to our country, and the assistance given by him to General Washington during his administration for the one great object, the independence and stability of the government of the United States, there is one thing in addition to the numerous proofs which I leave them and which I feel myself in duty bound to state, which is:

That a short time previous to General Washington's retiring from the presidency in the year 1796 General Hamilton suggested to him the idea of delivering a farewell address to the people on his withdrawal from public life, with the idea General Washington was well pleased, and in his answer to General Hamilton's suggestion gave him the heads on which he would wish to remark, with a request that Mr. Hamilton would prepare an address for him. Mr. Hamilton did so, and the address was written, principally at such times as his office was seldom frequented by his clients and visitors, and during the absence of his students to avoid interruption — at which times he was in the habit of calling me to sit with him, that he might read to me as he wrote in order, as he said, to discover how it sounded upon the ear, and making the remark, "My dear Eliza, you must be to me what Moliére's old nurse was to him."

The whole or nearly all the "Address" was read to me by him as he wrote it and a greater part if not all was written by him in my presence. The original was forwarded to General Washington, who approved of it with the exception of one paragraph of, I think, about four or five lines, which if I mistake not was on the subject of public schools, which was stricken out.

It was afterwards returned to Mr. Hamilton who made the desired alteration, and was afterwards delivered by General Washington and published in that form and has ever since been known as "General Washington's Farewell Address." Shortly after the publication of the address, my husband and myself were walking in Broadway when an old soldier accosted him with a request of him to purchase "General Washington's Farewell Address," which he did and, turning to me, said, "That man does not know he has asked me to purchase my own work."

The whole circumstances are at this moment so perfectly in my remembrance that I can call to mind his bringing General Washington's letter to me which returned the "Address" and remarking on the only alteration which he (General Washington) had requested to be made. [*Papers of Alexander Hamilton* 20:172-73]

1848 Washington, D.C.

[Interview by historian Benson J. Lossing for Chapter XIV, "The Last Surviving Belle of the Revolution," in his book *Hours with the Living Men and Women of the Revolution* (New York, 1889), 150-56, conducted in the Washington home she shared with her daughter, at "the close of 1848":]

She was then in her 92 year of her age and showing few symptoms in person or mind of extreme longevity. The sunny cheerfulness of her temper and quiet humor, which had shed their blessed influences around her all through life, still made her deportment genial and attractive. Her memory, faithful to the myriad impressions of a long and eventful experience, was ever ready with its various reminiscences to give a peculiar charm to her conversation upon subjects of the buried past. She was the then last living belle of the Revolution, and possibly the last survivor of the notable women who gave a charm to the Republican court at New York and Philadelphia during Washington's administration.

When I revealed to Mrs. Hamilton the object of my visit her eyes beamed with pleasurable emotion. She seated herself in an easy chair near me and we talked without ceasing upon the interesting theme until invited by her daughter to the tea table at eight oclock, where we were joined by a French lady, eight or ten years the junior of Mrs. Hamilton.

Our conversation began abruptly. "I have lately visited Judge [Gabriel] Ford at Morristown," I remarked.

"Judge Ford — Judge Ford," she repeated musingly. "Oh, I remember now! He called upon me a few years ago and brought to my recollection many little events which occurred while I was at Morristown with my father and mother during the war and which I had forgotten. I remember him as a bright boy, much thought of by Mr. Hamilton, who was then Washington's secretary. He brought to mama and me from Mrs. Washington an invitation to headquarters soon after our arrival at Morristown."

"Had you ever seen Mrs. Washington before?" I enquired.

"Never. She received us so kindly, kissing us both, for the general and papa were very warm friends. She was then almost fifty years old but was still handsome. She was quite short — a plump little woman with dark brown eyes, her hair a little frosty, and very plainly dressed for such a grand lady, as I considered her. She wore a plain, brown gown of homespun stuff, a large white neckerchief, a neat cap and her plain gold wedding ring, which she had worn more than twenty years. Her graces and cheerful manner delighted us. She was always my ideal of a true woman. Her thoughts were then much on the poor soldiers who had suffered during that dreadful winter, and she expressed her joy at the approach of a milder springtime."

"Were you much at headquarters afterward?" I enquired.

"Only a short time the next winter and an occasional visit," she replied. "We went to New Windsor after we were married, and there a few weeks afterward Mr. Hamilton left the general's military family [staff]. I made my home with my parents at Albany, while my husband remained in the army until after the surrender of Cornwallis. I visited Mrs. Washington at headquarters at Newburgh on her invitation in the summer of 1782, where I remember she had a beautiful flower garden planted and cultivated by her own hands.

"It was a lovely spot. The residence was an old stone house standing on the high bank of the river and overlooking a beautiful bay and the lofty highlands beyond. We were taken from Newburgh in a barge to the headquarters of the French army, a little below Peekskill, where we were cordially received by the Viscount de Noailles, a kinsman of Madame Lafayette, who was Mr. Hamilton's warm friend. We remained there several days and were witnesses of the excellent discipline of the French troops.

"There we saw the brave young Irish woman called 'Captain Molly,' whom I had seen two or three times before. She seemed to be a sort of pet of the French."

"Who was Captain Molly?" . . .

"Why, don't you remember reading of her exploit at the Battle of Monmouth? She was the wife of a cannoneer — a stout, redhaired, freckle-faced young Irish woman named Mary. While her husband was managing one of the field pieces in that action she constantly brought water from a spring nearby. A shot from the British killed him at his post, and the officer in command, having no one competent to fill his place, ordered the piece to be withdrawn.

"Molly (as she was called) saw her husband fall as she came from the spring and also heard the order. She dropped her bucket, seized the rammer, and vowed that she would fill the place of her husband and avenge his death. She performed the duty with great skill and won the admiration of all who saw her.

"My husband told me that she was brought in by General Greene the next morning, her dress soiled with blood and dust, and presented to Washington as worthy of reward. The General, admiring her courage, gave her the commission of sergeant and on his recommendation, her name was placed upon the list of half-pay officers for life.

"She was living near Fort Montgomery, in the Highlands, at the time of our visit and came to the camp two or three times while we were there. She was dressed in a sergeant's coat and waistcoat over her petticoat, and a cocked hat. The story of her exploit charmed the French officers and they made her many presents. She would sometimes pass along the French lines when on parade and get her hat nearly filled with half-crowns."

"You must have seen and became acquainted with very many of the most distinguished men and women of America, and also eminent foreigners, while your husband was in Washington's Cabinet," I remarked.

"Oh, yes," she replied. "I had little of private life in those days. Mrs. Washington who, like myself, had a passionate love of home and domestic life, often complained of the 'waste of time' she was compelled to endure. 'They call me that First Lady in the Land and think I must be extremely happy,' she would say almost bitterly at times and add, 'They might more properly call me the Chief State Prisoner.'

"As I was younger than she, I mingled more in the gaieties of the day. I was fond of dancing and usually attended the public balls that were given. I was at the inauguration ball — the most brilliant of them all — which was given early in May at the Assembly Rooms on Broadway, above Wall Street. It was attended by the President and Vice-President, the Cabinet officers, a majority of the members of Congress, the French and Spanish Ministers, and military and civil officers, with their wives and daughters.

"Mrs. Washington had not yet arrived in New York from Mount Vernon, and did not until three weeks later. On that occasion every woman who attended the ball was presented with a fan, prepared in Paris, with ivory frame and when open displayed a likeness of Washington in profile."

"Were you often at balls which Washington attended?" . . .

"Frequently."

"Did he usually dance on such occasions?"

"I never saw Washington dance. . . . He would always choose a partner and *walk* through the figure correctly, but he never danced. His favorite was the minuet, a slow, graceful dance suited to his dignity and gravity and now little known, I believe."

"Mrs. Washington's receptions were very brilliant, were they not?" . . .

"Brilliant so far as beauty, fashion, and social distinction went. . . . Otherwise they were very plain and entirely unostentatious."

"Did you usually attend them?" I asked.

"Frequently. I remember a very exciting scene at one of her earlier receptions. Ostrich plumes, waving high overhead, formed a part of the evening head-dress of a fashionable belle at that time. Miss McEvers, a sister of Mrs. Edward Livingston, who was present, had plumes unusually high. The ceiling of the drawing room of the President's house near Franklin Square was rather low, and Miss McEver's plumes were ignited by the flames of the chandelier. Major Jackson, Washington's aide-de-camp, sprang to the rescue of the young lady and extinguished the fire by smothering it with his hand."

"You saw many distinguished French people, refugees from the tempest of the Revolution in France, did you not?"

"Very many. New York became much Frenchified in speech and manners. Mr. Hamilton spoke French fluently, and as he did not sympathize with the revolutionists, who drove the exiles from their homes, he was a favorite with many of the cultivated *emigrés*.

"Among the most distinguished of these was Talleyrand, a strange creature, who stayed in America nearly two years. He was notoriously misshapen, lame in one foot, his manners far from elegant. The tone of his voice was disagreeable, and in dress he was rather slovenly. Mr. Hamilton saw much of him, and while he admired the shrewd diplomat for his great intellectual endowments, he detested his utter lack of principle. He had no conscience. In the summer of 1794 he spent several days with us at the Grange on Harlem Heights."

"Did you not entertain the young son of Lafayette and his tutor at the Grange a year or two later?" . . .

"We did, while they were waiting for Washington to retire from office. They came to this country when the Marquis was in an Austrian prison and his wife and daughter were gladly sharing his fate. Their son, George Washington, was sent to the protection of Lafayette's beloved friend.

"The President and Mrs. Washington would gladly have

received them into their family, but State policy forbad it at that critical time. The lad and his tutor passed a whole summer with us at the Grange. At length he and his [tutor] went to Philadelphia, lived quietly at private lodgings, and when the retired President and his family left the seat of Government for Mount Vernon, the tutor and the pupil accompanied them. When the young man and his father were in this country twenty-odd years ago, they very warmly greeted me, for the Marquis loved Mr. Hamilton as a brother. Their love was mutual." ...

At my request she kindly wrote her name in my notebook. I bade her adieu immediately after tea. Her sweet spirit departed on November 9th, 1854, after a pilgrimage on the earth of 97 years and 3 months.

NOTES

Notes to Deborah Read Franklin

1. Leonard W. Labaree, "Deborah Read Franklin," *Notable American Women*, (ed. E.T. James, 3 vols. (Cambridge: Harvard University Press, 1971). Subsequent sketch is based on Franklin's autobiography edited by Leo Lemay and me for the Norton Critical Edition (New York: Norton, 1986).

2. *Autobiography* 64-65.

2A. "Extracts from the Diary of Daniel Fisher," ed. Mrs. C.R. Howard, PMHB 17 (1893), 276-77.

3. Ibid 65.

4. September 6, 1758; Papers 8: 144. P.L. Ford, *Many-Sided Franklin* (N.Y.: Century, 1899), 275.

5. January 20, 1758; Ibid 8: 70 excerpts; LO 5425 complete.

6. October 8, 1765; *Papers* 12:300.

7. September 22, 1665; ibid 12:270.

8. January 12, 1766; ibid 13:32.

9. April 20-25, 1767; ibid 14:136.

10. August 16, 1770; ibid 17: 205-7.

11. October 3, 1770; ibid 17: 239.

12. November 20-27, 1769; ibid 16:231.

13. October 29, 1773; ibid 20: 450.

14. September 10, 1774; ibid 21:302.

15. Februrary 12, 1777; ibid 23:311.

16. December 7, 1778; ibid 28: 000; *Writings*, ed. J.A.L. Lemay (New York: Library of America, 1987), 925.

17. November 20-27, 1769; Papers 16:231.

Notes to Martha Washington

1. W.C. Ford, ed. *Writings of Washington* (New York: Putnam's, 1889-93), 13:497-501.

2. Benson J. Lossing, *Mary and Martha Washington* (New York: Harpers, 1886) 162.

3. John B. Trussel, Jr., *Birthplace of the American Army* (Harrisburg, PA: History and Museum Commission, 1976), 96-98 and *PMHB* 17:76.

4. Lossing, 165.

5. United Press International dispatch, *Los Angeles Times*, 22 April 1985.

6. Anne Hollingsworth Wharton, *Martha Washington* (New York: Charles Scribner, 1899), 112.

7. W.W. Abbot, ed., *Papers of George Washington, Colonial Series* (Charlottesville, 1988), 6: 316n., 349, 352n; HM 5244; J.C. Fitzpatrick, ed. *Writings of Washington*, 39 vols. (Washington: GPO, 1933-44), 2:334-6.

8. Stephen Decatur, Jr., *Private Affairs of George Washington from the Records and Accounts of Tobias Lear* (Boston: Houghton- Mifflin Co., 1933), 66.

9. Ibid; Wharton, 112.

10. James Thomas Flexner, *Washington the Indispensable Man* (Boston: Little, Brown, 1974), 52.

11. Elizabeth Ambler Carrington q. in "Some New Washington Relics," *Century 40* (May 1890) 16-18; dated 27 November 1799.

12. Wharton, 56.

13. Lossing, 126-7.

14. Wharton, 90.

15. George Washington to LaFayette, 15 November 1781; *Fitzpatrick*, 23:340.

16. Wharton, 156.

17. Ibid, 164.

18. Max Farrand, ed. *Records of the Federal Convention of 1787* (New Haven: Yale University Press, 1911, 1937), 3:302.

19. Martha Washington to Mercy Otis Warren, 26 November 1789, HM 18781 q. in Lossing 280, Wharton 203.

20. Ibid.

21. Wharton, 192.

22. Lossing, 271.

23. Wharton, 203.

24. "No, God forbid" is in HM 18781 only; not in Wharton or Lossing.

25. Lossing's interview with Mrs. Hamilton, *Hours with the Living Men and Women of the Revolution* (New York: Funk and Wagnalls, 1899), 151.

26. June 1794 Privately Printed, W.K. Bixby, 1922.

27. Miriam Anne Bourne, *First Family* (New York: Norton, 1982), 193.

28. Ibid.

29. Charles Moore, *Family Life of George Washington* (Boston: Houghton-Mifflin, 1926), 164.

30. R.W.G. Vail, ed. "A Dinner at Mount Vernon from the Unpublished Journal of Joshua Brooks," *New York Historical Society Quarterly* 31(April 1947), [72-85] 74, 81.

32. Obituary, *Pennsylvania Gazette*, 2 June 1802.

Notes to Grace Galloway

1. Lewis Burd Walker, ed. *The Burd Papers* (Philadelphia: privately printed, 1899), 13-14.

2. Harold D. Eberlein and C.V. Hubbard, Portrait of a Colonial City (Philadelphia: Lippincott, 1939), 74.

3. Lillian Miller, ed. *Select Papers of Charles Willson Peale* (New Haven: Yale University Press, 1983), 291.

4. Diary of Grace Growdon Galloway, ed. Raymond C. Werner (New York: Arno Press, 1971), 51-53 covers the eviction; subsequent references are to this edition.

5. Page 32.

6. HM 36845: 6 November 1753.

7. Eberlein, 74; Benjamin H. Newcomb, *Franklin and Galloway* (New Haven: Yale University Press, 1972), 225. Mrs. Galloway's nightmares are recorded in the diary for 31 August and 20 September 1779 (pp. 179, 187). My speculations on Samuel Griffen are based on standard genealogical

and military resources; and on *William and Mary Quarterly* 7 (1898) 60.

8. May 22, 1779, HM 36846.

9. Page 57.

10. HM 36846.

11. William H. Rawle, "Laurel Hill," *PMHB* 35(1911) 401-403.

12. Page 76.

13. Quoted in Mary Beth Norton, *Liberty's Daughters* (Boston: Little, Brown, 1980), 44-45.

14. Deborah Morris to Joseph Galloway, 29 May 1782; HM 36871.

15. Horace Binney, *Reports of Cases Adjudged in the Supreme Court of Pennsylvania*, 3 vols (Philadelphia: Farrand, 1809), 1:1-2.

16. William H. Davis, *History of Bucks County* (Doylestown: Democrat, 1876), 148.

17. *Burke's Irish Family Records* s v Manwaring-Burton. See also Elizabeth Evans, *Weathering the Storm: Women of the American Revolution* (New York: Scribners, 1975), 185-244.

Notes to Abigail Adams

1. *Adams Family Correspondence*, ed. L.H. Butterfield, 4 vols. (Cambridge: Harvard University Press, 1963), 1: 45; 7 May 1764. References to this source are abbreviated AFC; its text modernized.

2. AFC 1: 47; 9 May 1764.

3. AFC 1: 338; 18 April 1776.

4. *Letters of Mrs. Adams*, ed. Charles Francis Adams, 4th ed., (Boston: Wilkins, Carter, 1848), 358, hereafter abbreviated CFA.

5. Ibid.

6. CFA 402; 5 June 1809.

7. AFC 1: 370; 31 March 1776; see also 402: "Whilst you are proclaiming peace and good will to men, emancipating all nations, you insist upon retaining an absolute power over

wives." She goes on to tease him saying, in effect, we may appear to be submitting but do not push us too far — "We have it in our power not only to free ourselves but to subdue our masters, and without violence throw both your natural and legal authority at your feet," 7 May 1776.

8. Ibid 310; 22 October 1775.

9. CFA 402; 5 June 1809.

10. AFC 2: 306; 11 August 1777.

11. CFA 402; 5 June 1809.

12. Caroline Smith de Windt, ed., *Journal and Correspondence of Miss Adams*, 2 vols. (New York: 1841), 2: 228. The editor was the granddaughter Caroline, correspondent of Abigail Adams in her old age.

13. AFC 4:256; 9 December 1781.

14. *Papers of Thomas Jefferson*, ed. Julian Boyd (Princeton: Princeton University Press, 1950-), 12: 625.

15. CFA 199-200.

16. *Notable American Women*, ed. Edward T. James (Cambridge: Harvard University Press, 1971), 1:8. The entry, by L.H. Butterfield, editor of the Adams papers, is the best sketch of Abigail Adams's life; pages 6-9.

17. CFA 357; 20 March 1791.

18. See AFC 3; xxviii; CFA 387; 16 June 1803, on hesitating to write.

19. CFA 389; 20 May 1804.

20. *Notable American Women*, 1:8; 8 December 1804.

21. Allyn B. Forbes, ed., "Abigail Adams, Commentator," *Proceedings of the Massachusetts Historical Society* 66(1936-41):143; 29 August 1808.

22. Ibid.

23. *New Letters of Abigail Adams*, ed. Stewart Mitchell (Boston: Houghton Mifflin, 1947), 23; 1 September 1789.

24. Caroline Smith de Windt, ed., 1:216; 2 February 1809.

27. Ibid, 1:229; 23 October 1814.

28. Ibid, 1:239; 1 January 1820.

29. Quoted from Adams Papers microfilm, reel 361, in Edith Belle Gelles, "Abigail Adams: Domesticity and the American Revolution," PhD Dissertation, University of California at Irvine, 1978, 185.

30. *Diary of William Bentley*, 4 vols (Salem: Essex Institute, 1914), 4:556-557; 30 October 1818; q. also in NAW 9.

Notes to Molly Morris

1. Walter H. Stowe, ed., *Life & Letters of Bishop William White* (New York: Morehouse, 1937), 8.

2. Ibid, 7; cf Thomas Harrington Montgomery, *Account of the Meeting of Descendents of Colonel Thomas White* (Philadelphia: privately printed, 1879) and Charles Henry Hart, "Mary White — Mrs. Robert Morris," *Pennsylvania Magazine of History and Biography* 2(1878) 157-62 also reprinted by Montgomery; these along with Morris manuscripts in the Huntington Library, signified by the prefix HM, provided the basic biographical data.

3. *PMHB* 16(1892) 247.

4. William Brotherhead, "Robert Morris" in *Eminent Philadelphians*, ed. Henry Simpson (Philadelphia: Brotherhead, 1859), 706 quoting letter by Samual Breck, 12 January 1818.

5. Montgomery 53.

6. Ibid, 55.

7. Ibid, 57.

8. *PMHB* 35 (1911) 398.

9. *Travels in North America by the Marquis de Chastellux*, ed. H.C. Rice, Jr. (Chapel Hill: Univ. North Carolina Press, 1963), 164; PMHB 1(1877) 224.

10. Elizabeth Ellet, *Queens of American Society* (Philadelphia: 1867), 52.

11. July 17, 1783; HM 13516 — Tommy "seem'd to think the request rather large as he had other correspondents, and therefore did not positively acquiesce in the proposal, at least as to the frequency."

12. January 5, 1783; HM 13513.

13. December 19, 1786; HM 13530.

14. January 13, 1788; HM 13528.

15. Montgomery, 165.

16. December 12, 1787; HM 13553.

17. Brotherhead, 710; Albert J. Beveridge, *John Marshall*, 2 vols (Boston: Houghton Mifflin, 1916), 2: 202n.

18. Ethel E. Rasmussen, "Democratic Environment-Aristocratic Aspiration," *PMHB* 90(1966): 180.

19. *PMHB* 23 (1899): 309.

20. Montgomery 177; cf HM 13611 dated 11 November 1798.

21. [June 1798] HM 13624.

22. October 10, 1798; HM 13622.

23. September 7, 1799; HM 13628.

24. Brotherhead 715.

25. 31 January 1805; HM 13629.

26. Montgomery 182.

27. Ibid 183.

Notes to Sally Jay

1. *John Jay: Unpublished Papers*, ed. Richard B. Morris, 2 vols. (New York: Harper & Row, 1975, 1980), 2: 644; 18 November 1783. Subsequently abbreviated JJUP, or simply volume and page.

2. 1:517; 28-30 December 1778.

3. 1:124; January 1773.

4. 1:467; 12 March 1778.

5. 1:380; 23-24 March 1777.

6. 1:437; 18 August 1777.

7. 2:189-91; 24 June 1781; 2:197; 25 July 1781.

8. 1:683; 12-26 December 1776.

9. *Queens of American Society*, ed. E. Ellet (New York: Scribners, 1867), 52; the entry by grandson John Jay.

10. JJUP 2:178; 14 March 1781.

11. 1:692-3; 4 March 1780.

12. 2:476; 14 November 1782.

13. Frank Monaghan, *John Jay* (Indianapolis: Bobbs-Merrill, 1935), 217.

14. JJUP 2:476; 14 November 1782.

15. Bernard Mayo, "A Peppercorn for Mr. Jefferson," *Virginia Quarterly Review* 19 (1943): 230, quoting Latrobe to

his wife, 30 November 1802.

16. JJUP 2:663-4; 11 December 1783.

17. Monaghan 266.

18. *Papers of Thomas Jefferson*, ed. Julian Boyd (Princeton: Princeton University Press, 1950-), 14:291; 25 November 1788.

19. [Caroline Smith de Wendt, ed.] *Correspondence of Miss Adams* (New York: Wiley and Putnam, 1842), 2 vols, 2:74; 20 May 1788.

20. Monaghan, 320.

21. *Queens of American Society*, 78; 2 May 1794.

22. HM 26901; 20 December 1794.

23. *Correspondence and Public Papers of John Jay*, ed. Henry P. Johnston, 4 vols (New York: Putnam, 1890-93), 3:431; 10 June 1792.

24. HM 26901; 20 December 1794.

25. *Queens of American Society*, 84.

Notes to Nancy Morris

1. Max M. Mintz, *Gouverneur Morris and the American Revolution* (Norman: University of Oklahoma Press, 1970), 139-41.

2. Richard B. Morris, ed. *John Jay: the Making of a Revolutionary* (New York: Harper and Row, 1975), 788, 821.

3. Howard Swiggett, *The Extraordinary Mr. Morris* (Garden City: Doubleday, 1952), 397. This is the source for many letters cited below, along with William Cabell Bruce, *John Randolph of Roanoke*, 2 vols (New York: Putnam, 1922). Transcripts of depositions are in *The Papers of John Marshall*, eds. Charles T. Cullen and Hebert A. Johnson (Chapel Hill: University of North Carolina Press, 1977) 2: 161-78.

4. Marshall 163-66; *Virginia Gazette*, 3 April 1793, p. 3.

5. Swiggett 397.

6. Ibid 397.

7. Bruce 2:300.

8. Swiggett 426.

9. Ibid 380.

10. Ibid 425.
11. Bruce 2:277-78.
12. Swiggett 426.
13. Bruce 2:296. Her entire letter is reprinted here along with Randolph's, pp. 274-295.
14. Mintz 240.
15. Swiggett 440.
16. Bruce 2:772.
17. Swiggett 441.
18. Bruce 2:299.
19. *New York Times*, 15 August 1953, 15:3.

Notes to Martha Jefferson Randolph

1. To Marquis Barbé de Marbois, 5 December 1783, *Papers*, ed. Julian Boyd (Princeton: Princeton University Press, 1952), 6:374; cf William H. Gaines, Jr., *Thomas Mann Randolph* (Baton Rouge: Louisiana State University Press, 1966), v.

2. Sarah N. Randolph, "Mrs. Thomas Mann Randolph," in *Worthy Women of our First Century*, ed. Sarah Wister and Agnes Irwin (Philadelphia: Lippincott, 1877), 10. This sixty-page biographical sketch by her grand-daughter has been the basis for mine, supplemented by more recent documents.

3. Henry S. Randall, *Thomas Jefferson*, 3 vols. (New York: Derby and Jackson, 1858), 1: 63n.

4. *Papers*, 3:532-533n; Page Smith, *John Wilson*, 212.

5. Sarah N. Randolph, *Domestic Life of Thomas Jefferson* (rpt Cambridge: Harvard University Press, 1939), 42; Randall, 1:381.

6. Hamilton Wilcox Pierson, "Private Life of Thomas Jefferson," *Jefferson at Monticello*, ed. James A. Bear, Jr. (Charlottesville: University Press of Virginia, 1967), 99-100.

7. To Marquis de Chastellux, 26 November 1782, *Papers*, 6:203.

8. Ibid, 199-200n.

9. Randolph, *Worthy Women*, 14.

10. Papers, 11:282; 9 April 1787.

11. Randolph, *Worthy Women*, 15.

12. Papers 13:347.

13. Ibid, 11:240.

14. Randolph, *Worthy Women*, 22.

15. Ibid, 23-24.

16. Edward M. Betts and James A Bear, Jr., eds., *Family Letters of Thomas Jefferson* (Columbia: University of Missouri Press, 1966), 52.

17. Randolph, *Worthy Women*, 25, where the date should be "early in the year 1797," cf Betts and Bear, 141 for Jefferson's reply.

18. *Dolley Madison Life and Letters*, ed. Allen C. Clark (Washington: W.F. Roberts, 1914), 105; 1 September 1809.

19. Randolph, *Domestic Life*, 259.

20. Randolph, *Worthy Women*, 43; Betts and Bear, 193.

21. Margaret Bayard Smith, *Forty Years of Washington Society*, ed. Gaillard Hunt (London: Unwin, 1906), 76, 396.

22. Gaines, *Thomas Mann Randolph*, 184, 187.

23. Betts and Bear, 253; 14 January 1804.

24. Margaret Bayard Smith, 309.

25. Randolph, *Worthy Women*, 55.

26. Ibid, 56.

27. Randolph, *Domestic Life*, 370.

Notes to Dolley Madison

1. Huntington Library manuscript BN422; Anna Maria Thornton to Clara Baldwin, 13 March 1814.

2. Constance Green, *Washington Village and Capital*, 2 vols (Princeton: Princeton University Press, 1962), 1:148.

3. *Letters of Mary Boardman Crowninshield*, ed. F.B. Crowninshield (Cambridge, Mass.: Riverside Press, 1905), 24.

4. Ibid, 35.

5. *Letters of Washington Irving*, ed. R.W. Alderman, 4 vols. (Boston: Twayne, 1978-82), 1:297.

6. *Diary of Elbridge Gerry, Jr.*, ed. Claude G. Bowers (New York: Brentano's, 1927), 178.

7. Wendy Buehr, *American Manners and Morals* (New York: American Heritage, 1969), 83.

8. Irving Brant, *James Madison*, 6 vols (Indianapolis: Bobbs-Merrill, 1950-61), 5:29.

9. Ibid 6:135; cf Allen C. Clark, *Life and Letters of Dolly Madison* (Washington: Roberts, 1914), 147-148.

10. Conover Hunt-Jones, *Dolley and the "Great Little Madison"* (Washington: American Institute of Architects, 1977), 12. This is the basic biographical source for this profile.

11. Ibid, 13; 10 April 1811.

12. "Diary of Frances Few," ed. N.E. Cunningham, Jr., *Journal of Southern History*, 29(1963), 351-352.

13. Allen C. Clark, "Dr. and Mrs. William Thornton," *Records of the Columbia Historical Society*, 18(1915), 178; 4 June 1805.

14. Margaret Bayard Smith, *Forty Years in Washington Society*, ed. Gaillard Hunt (London: Unwin, 1906), 62; March 1809.

15. Ibid, 63.

16. Conover Hunt-Jones, 33.

17. Brant, 6:27.

18. Conover Hunt-Jones, 45.

19. J. Hall Pleasants, "Four Landscape Painters," *Proceedings of the American Antiquarian Society*, 52(1942), 312-313.

20. Conover Hunt-Jones, 50.

21. Ibid.

22. Ralph Ketcham, *James Madison* (New York: Macmillan, 1971), 670.

23. Paul G. Sifton, "What a Dreadful Prospect," *PMBH*, 87(1963), 182-188; the will is reprinted in Carl Holliday, *Women's Life in Colonial Days* (Boston: Cornhill, 1922), 297-298.

24. *Papers of James Madison*, ed. Robert Rutland (Chicago: Chicago University Press, 1962-), 15:357.

25. Huntington Library manuscript HM 31360; Elizabeth Chilton Bowdon to Frances Jane Chilton Rice, 2 January 1847.

26. Oliver Perry Chitwood, *John Tyler, Champion of the Old South* (New York: Appleton-Century, 1939), 392 and note.

27. Jessie Benton Frémont, *Souvenirs of My Time* (Boston: Lothrop, 1887), 112.

28. Ibid, 111.

29. J. Madison Cutts, "Dolley Madison," *Records of the Columbia Historical Society*, 3(1900) 28-72, 50.

Notes to Elizabeth Schuyler Hamilton

1. Joseph Schafer, "High Society in Pioneer Wisconsin," *Wisconsin Magazine of History* 20(1936) 449.

2. "Adéle DeP. Gratiot's Narrative," *Collections of the State Historical Society of Wisconsin* 10(1885[1909]) 275.

3. See Paul M. Angle, *"Here I Have Lived," a History of Lincoln's Springfield 1821-1865* (New Brunswick: Rutgers UP, 1935) 14-15.

4. Broadus Mitchell, *Alexander Hamilton, the National Adventure* (NY: Macmillan, 1962) 554.

5. Local legends are surveyed in Harold D. Eberlein, *Manor and Historic Homes of the Hudson Valley* (Philadelphia: Lippincott, 1924), 229-34.

6. Ibid 230.

7. Allan M. Hamilton, *Intimate Life of Alexander Hamilton* (NY: Scribners, 1910) 95; Oswald Tilghman, ed., *Tench Tilghman's Memoirs* (Albany, privately printed, 1876), 90.

8. *Papers of Alexander Hamilton*, ed. Harold C. Syrett, 27 vols, (NY: Columbia University Press, 1961-87), 2:38. In this jocular letter of April 1779, he listed among qualities he insisted upon in a wife that she be young, handsome, sensible, well bred, chaste, generous. "She must believe in god and hate a saint. But as to fortune, the larger stock of that the better" (37).

9. June 30, 1780; Papers 2: 348.

10. Hamilton, *Intimate Life* 126-127.

11. January 21, 1781; *Papers* 2:539n.

12. March 28, 1791; Bernard C. Steiner, *Life and Cor-*

respondence of James McHenry (Cleveland: Burrows, 1907), 129.

13. *Papers* 10: 377-79; the pamphlet of August 1797 is reprinted in 21: 215-85.

14. Mitchell, *Alexander Hamilton*, 418-22.

15. July 13, 1797; *Papers* 21: 163.

16. Ben Perley Poore, *Reminiscences of 60 Years in the National Metropolis*, 2 vols (Philadelphia: Hubbard, 1886) 1: 169.

17. Hamilton, *Intimate Life*, 416-20.

18. George W. Bethune, ed. *Memoirs of Mrs. Joanna Bethune* (New York: Harpers, 1863) 111.

19. Hamilton, *Intimate Life* 113; *Proceedings of Massachusetts Historical Society* 46 (1913) 338.

20. Victor Hugo Paltsis, *Washington's Farewell Address* (New York: New York Public Library, 1935) reprints manuscripts and relevant documents; cf *Papers* 20: 172-73.

21. A committee of the Historical Society of Pennsylvania appointed in February 1826 issued a documented report of the controversy to that time; *Memoirs of the Historical Society. . .* 1(1864) 241-67. They concluded that Hamilton merely copied the address.

22. To be published after her death, the affidavit is reprinted in Hamilton, *Intimate Life* 110-12; the Miliére allusion is to the *Spectator* number 70, first published 21 May 1711 and many times reprinted.

23. *Papers of James Madison*, ed. C.F. Hobson, et al (Chicago: University of Chicago Press; Charlottesville, University Press of Virginia, 1962-) 12: 120-21n, 133-34n.

24. Hamilton, *Intimate Life* 116-117.

25. Marian Gouverneur, *As I Remember* (New York: Appleton, 1911) 193, 197.

26. Ed. Allan Nevins (New York: Longmans, Green, 1929) 52.

27. "Reminiscences of Mrs. John M. Binckley," *Records of Columbia Historical Society* 30(1928)353; Jessie Benton Frémont, *Souvenirs of My Time* (Boston: Lothrop, 1887), 119.

28. Benson J. Lossing interview, "at the close of 1848," reprinted in his *Hours with the Living Men and Women of the*

Revolution (New York: Funk and Wagnalls, 1889) 146-56.

    29. Ibid, 151.

    30. Ibid, 153.

    31. Page 149.

    32. *Sacramento Guide Book* (Sacramento: Sacramento Bee, 1939), 96-97.

    33. Jesse Fremont, *Souvenirs* 119.

BIBLIOGRAPHY

Adams, Abigail. *Letters.* Edited by Charles Francis Adams. Fourth ed. Boston: Wilkins, Carter, 1848.
— *New Letters.* Edited by Stewart Mitchell. Boston: Houghton-Mifflin, 1947.
Bentley, William. *Diary.* 4 vols. Salem: Essex Institute, 1914.
Bethune, Joanna. *Memoirs.* Edited by G.W. Bethune. New York: Harpers, 1863.
Binney, Horace. *Reports of Cases Adjudged in the Supreme Court of Pennsylvania.* 3 vols. Philadelphia: Farrand, 1809.
Bourne, Miriam Anne. *First Family.* New York: Norton, 1982.
Brant, Irving. *James Madison.* 6 vols. Indianapolis: Bobbs Merrill, 1950-61.
Brinckley, Mrs. John M. "Some Reminiscences." *Records of the Columbia Historical Society* 30 (1928): 343-53.
Brooks, Joshua. "A Dinner at Mount Vernon." *New York State Historical Society Quarterly* 31 (1947): 72-85.
Brotherhead, William. "Robert Morris." In *Eminent Philadelphians.* Edited by Henry Simpson. Philadelphia: Brotherhead, 1859.
Bruce, William Cabell. *John Randolph of Roanoke.* 2 vols. New York: Putnam, 1922.
Buehre, Wendy. *American Manners and Morals.* New York: American Heritage, 1969.
Butterfield, Lyman H. *Adams Family Correspondence.* Cambridge: Harvard University Press, 1963.
Chitwood, Oliver Perry. *John Tyler.* New York: Appleton- Century, 1939.
Clark, Allen C. "Dr. and Mrs. Thornton." In *Records of the Columbia Historical Society*, 18 (1915): 144-208.

— *Life and Letters of Dolly Madison".* Washington: Roberts, 1914.

Crowninshield, Mary Boardman. *Letters.* Edited by F.B. Crowninshield. Cambridge: Riverside Press, 1905.

Cutts, J. Madison. "Dolley Madison." In *Records of the Columbia Historical Society,* 3 (1900): 28-72.

Davis, William H. *History of Bucks County.* Doylestown: Democrat, 1876.

Decatur, Stephen. *Private Affairs of George Washington.* Boston: Houghton Mifflin, 1933.

Eberlein, Harold D. *Manor and Historic Homes of the Hudson Valley.* Philadelphia: Lippincott, 1924.

— and C.V. Hubbard. *Portrait of a Colonial City.* Philadelphia: Lippincott, 1939.

Ellet, Elizabeth. *Queens of American Society.* Philadelphia: Scribners, 1867.

Evans, Elizabeth. *Weathering the Storm.* New York: Scribners, 1975.

Farrand, Max. *Recors of the Federal Convention of 1787* New Haven: Yale University Press, 1911, 1937.

Few, Frances. "Diary 1808-9." Edited by N.E. Cunningham, Jr. *Journal of Southern History,* 29 (1963): 344-61.

Fisher, Daniel. "Extracts from the Diary . . . . 1755." *Pennsylvania Magazine of History and Biography,* 17(1893): 263-78.

Flexner, James Thomas. *Washington the Indispensable Man.* Boston: Little, Brown, 1974.

Forbes, Allyn B. "Abigail Adams Commentator." *Proceedings of the Massachusetts Historical Society,* 66 (1936-41): 143.

Ford, Paul L. *The Many-Sided Benjamin Franklin.* New York: Century, 1899.

Franklin, Benjamin. *Autobiography.* Edited by J.A.L. Lemay and P.M. Zall. New York: Norton, 1986.

— *Papers.* Edited by L.W. Labaree, et. al. New Haven: Yale University Press, 1959- .

— *Writings.* Edited by J.A.L. Lemay. New York: Library of America, 1987.

Frémont, Jessie Benton. *Souvenirs of My Time.* Boston:

Lothrop, 1887.

Gaines, William H., Jr. *Thomas Mann Randolph*. Baton Rouge: Louisiana State University Press, 1966.

Galloway, Grace Growdon. *Diary*. Edited by Raymond C. Weaver. New York: Arno, 1971.

Gerry, Elbridge, Jr. *Diary*. Edited by Claude G. Bowers. New York: Brenano's, 1927.

Gouverneur, Marian. *As I Remember*. New York: Appleton, 1911.

Gratiot, Adéle. "Narrative." *Collections of the State Historical Society of Wisconsin*, 10(1885): 261-75.

Green, Constance. *Washington Village and Capital*. 2 vols. Princeton: Princeton University Press, 1962.

Hamilton, Alexander. *Papers*. Edited by H.C. Syrett. 27 vols. New York: Columbia University Press, 1961-87.

Hamilton, Allan M. *Intimate Life of Alexander Hamilton*. New York: Scribners, 1910.

Hamilton, James A. *Reminiscences*. New York: Scribners, 1869.

Hart, Charles Henry. "Mary White." *Pennsylvania Magazine of History and Biography*, 2(1878): 157-62.

Holliday, Carl. *Women's Life in Colonial Days*. Boston: Cornhill, 1922.

Hunt-Jones, Conover. *Dolley and "the Great Little Madison."* Washington: American Institute of Architects, 1977.

Irving, Washington. *Letters*. Edited by R.W. Alderman. 4 vols. Boston: Twayne, 1978-82.

James, E.T., ed. *Notable American Women*. 3 vols. Cambridge: Harvard University Press, 1971.

Jay, John. *Correspondence and Public Papers*. Edited by H.P. Johnson. 4 vols. New York: Putnams, 1890-93.

— *Unpublished Papers*. Edited by R.B. Morris, 2 vols. New York: Harper and Row, 1975, 1980.

Jefferson, Thomas. *Family Letters*. Edited by E.M. Betts and J.A. Bear, Jr. Columbia: University of Missouri Press, 1966.

— *Papers*. Edited by Julian Boyd. Princeton: Princeton University Press, 1950- .

Ketcham, Ralph. *James Madison*. New York: Macmillan, 1971.

Lopez, C.A. and E.W. Herbert, *The Private Franklin*. New York: Norton, 1975.

Lossing, Benson J. *Hours with the Living Men and Women of the Revolution*. New York: Funk and Wagnalls, 1889.

— *Mary and Martha Washington*. New York: Harpers, 1886.

McHenry, James. *Life and Correspondence*. Edited by Bernard C. Steiner. Cleveland: Burrows, 1907.

Madison, James. *Papers*. Edited by C.F. Hobson, et al. Chicago: University of Chicago Press; Charlottesville: University Press of Virginia, 1962 - .

Mayo, Bernard. "A Peppercorn for Mr. Jefferson." In *Virginia Quarterly Review*, 19(1943): 222-35.

Mintz, Max M. *Gouverneur Morris and the American Revolution*. Norman: University of Oklahoma Press, 1970.

Mitchell, Broadus. *Alexander Hamilton, the National Adventure*. New York: Macmillan, 1962.

Monaghan, Frank. *John Jay*. Indianapolis: Bobbs Merrill, 1935.

Montgomery, Thomas H. *Account of the Meeting of Descendants of Colonel Thomas White*. Philadelphia: privately printed, 1879.

Moore, Charles. *Family Life of George Washington*. Boston: Houghton Mifflin, 1926.

Newcomb, Benjamin H. *Franklin and Galloway*. New Haven: Yale University Press, 1972.

Norton, Mary Beth. *Liberty's Daughters*. Boston: Little Brown, 1980.

Peale, Charles Willson. *Select Papers* Edited by Lillian Miller. 2 vols. New Haven: Yale University Press, 1983.

Pierson, Hamilton W. "Private Life of Thomas Jefferson." In *Jefferson at Monticello*. Edited by J.A. Bear, Jr. Charlottesville: University Press of Virginia, 1967.

Pleasants, J. Hall. "Four Landscape Painters." *Proceedings of the American Antiquarian Society*, 52(1942): 186-324.

Polk, James. *Diary*. Edited by Allan Nevins. New York: Longmans Green, 1929.

Poore, Ben Perley. *Reminiscences of 60 Years in the National Metropolis.* 2 vols. Philadelphia: Hubbard, 1886.

Randolph, Sarah N. "Mrs. Thomas Mann Randolph." In *Worthy Women of Our First Century.* Edited by Sarah Wister and Agnes Irwin. Philadelphia: Lippincott, 1877.

Rasmussen, Ethel E. "Democrat Environment - Aristocratic Aspiration." *Pennsylvania Magazine of History and Biography,* 90(1966): 155-82.

Sacramento Bee. *Sacramento Guide Book.* Sacramento: Bee, 1939.

Schafer, Joseph. "High Society in Pioneer Wisconsin". *Wisconsin Magazine of History,* 20 (1936-37): 446-61.

Sifton, Paul G. "What a Dreadful Prospect." *Pennsylvania Magazine of History and Biography,* 87(1963): 182-88.

Smith, Abigail Adams. *Journal and Correspondence.* 2 vols. Edited by Caroline Smith de Windt. New York: Wiley and Putnam, 1841-42.

Smith, Margaret Bayard. "Dolley Madison." In *National Portrait Gallery.* Philadelphia: Herrick and Longacre, 1836.

— *Forty Years of Washington Society.* Edited by Gaillard Hunt. London: Unwin, 1906.

Swiggett, Howard. *The Extraordinary Mr. Morris.* Garden City: Doubleday, 1952.

Tilghman, Tench. *Memoirs.* Edited by Oswald Tilghman. Albany: privately printed, 1876.

Trussell, John B., Jr. *Birthplace of the American Army.* Harrisburg PA: History and Museum Commission, 1976.

Upton, Harriet T. *Our Early Presidents, Their Wives and Children.* Boston: Lothrop, 1890.

Walker, Lewis Burd, ed. *The Burd Papers.* Philadelphia: privately printed, 1899.

Washington, George. *Farewell Address.* Edited by V.H. Paltsis. New York: New York Public Library, 1935.

Papers. Edited by W.W. Abbot, et al. Charlottesville: University Press of Virginia, 1983- .

Writings. Edited by J.C. Fitzpatrick. 39 vols. Washington: Government Printing Office, 1933.

Writings. Edited by W.C. Ford. 14 vols. New York: Putnams, 1889-93.

Wharton, Anne Hollingsworth. *Martha Washington.* New York: Scribners, 1899.

White, William. *Life and Letters.* Edited by W.H. Stowe. New York: Morehouse, 1937.

INDEX